A CHILD
BORN MAN

KENNETH H. THOMPSON

iUniverse, Inc.
Bloomington

A Child Born Man

iUniverse books may be ordered through booksellers or by contacting:

iUniverse
1663 Liberty Drive
Bloomington, IN 47403
www.iuniverse.com
1-800-Authors (1-800-288-4677)

ISBN: 978-1-4759-2281-3 (sc)
ISBN: 978-1-4759-2283-7 (hc)
ISBN: 978-1-4759-2282-0 (ebk)

Printed in the United States of America

iUniverse rev. date: 05/15/2012

Author's Note

A Child Born Man—my life story—is the only book that I've written so far. I started it in the early 1970s when I left New York City to escape the darkness in my life and went to work as a lobby porter. I was able to complete my story over the last few years, thanks to help from a student editor I hired by the hour at a college where I worked and to technology. The process of writing this book has taught me much about life.

INTRODUCTION

Kenneth was five when it all started. His mother loved him very much, and the male "father figure" who was around didn't even care whether or not he existed. From the perspective of hindsight, it is clear that this man, Rich, mistreated Kenneth because the boy wasn't his son. The child was never right as far as Rich was concerned.

Kenneth's mother told him that his father was dead—that he had died when a gasoline truck he was driving was in an explosive accident. Kenneth was his mother's first boy. He had two brothers and two sisters whom he loved very much. The two sisters had a different father, and they were also mistreated by Rich. Rich seemed to have been sent by the devil himself with the sole purpose of destroying these children's and their mother's lives.

Rich was Anne's third of four boyfriends. Her first marriage, to Patty and Rita's father, had ended in a divorce. Kenneth's father was her second husband. Then came Rich—straight from hell.

During early childhood, Kenneth was like a father to his little brothers, Danny and Reggie. As far as Kenneth's sisters were concerned, Patty was very protective of Kenneth and Rita was always picking on him, but they all loved one another as brothers and sisters. Rita was also playful, thinking up and supervising different kinds of games for the children.

This story of these children's lives is very exciting. Without a dull moment, it will take you on a journey of emotions—it is sad, loving, touching, dangerous, emotional, enlightening, and spiritual. I hope that readers enjoy reading this inspirational story as much as I enjoyed writing it.

PART ONE

A LITTLE BOY HURT

"Kenneth, don't you have anything else to do but sit in that chair playing with your grandfather's pipe?" These were the first words that came out of Rich's mouth.

Frightened by the roar of this man's voice, Kenneth ran into his room. Even though he hadn't done anything wrong, the little boy, still a baby at the age of five, stayed quiet, not making any noise for fear that the man would come into the room and start more trouble with him. Kenneth searched in his dresser drawer for some crayons; he wanted to draw pictures of the different animals that he loved the most. His favorite animal to draw was his cat, Tiger, which he had found under a car one day in the rain, frightened, just as he was. They had both been scared—Kenneth because he was a little boy who loved his mother's boyfriend, though this scary man didn't love him, and Tiger because he'd been left alone in the rain.

"Honk, beep." Tears had been about to fall from Kenneth's eyes because of Rich's yelling. But they stopped now when he heard this sound—the sound of a smaller boy moving down the long hallway and getting closer to his room. Kenneth had padded down that long hallway many times, going to bed without supper. Now, a toy car came to a stop in front of the door. A knock followed, and Kenneth, knowing who it was, opened the door quietly.

"Can my car and I come in and get some gas out of the drawer?" the three-year-old asked.

Kenneth laughed. "Danny, how are you going to get gas out of the drawer?" he asked.

"Well," he replied, "my car ran out of gas, and I asked Patty where I could fill up the car with some gas. She said, 'Danny if you must play with that big, dumb-looking thing, you can fill it up in the bedroom drawer—the one you and Kenneth sleep in when you're bad.'" Patty had told Danny that she and Rita, who was age nine, only had playhouses, with dolls and lots of little girl things—"no gas for your stupid car." She had suggested he fill up with crayons or go to their mother's room and get some perfume to fill the car up with.

Kenneth knew that Mommy's perfume wouldn't be the answer to little Danny's problem, but to please the little boy, he went up to his mother's room to see what he could find. Once in the room, he found himself in another world, not realizing what he was doing. With crayons in his hands, he started, unaware, drawing on his mother's walls. And in his other hand, he was pouring expensive perfume all over the room. Kenneth had completely forgotten about little Danny's fantasy of filling up the car with perfume, which would have caused the same problem that he had caused himself. He was in another world, until he suddenly felt two strong hands roughly squeezing his shoulder blades. He instantly knew whose hands they were. Kenneth's guess was right, because, as he was spun around, he looked up into the cold and dark eyes of Satan himself—Rich.

What is going to happen now? thought the little boy. *Is he going to kill me and tell my mother that I ran away because of what I did in her room?*

"You little piece of garbage!" Rich screamed. "Your punishment for what you did is going to make you remember. Everyone else will be eating chicken for dinner. If you're hungry, you can suck the marrow out of the bones that we throw at you while you're chained to the chair—but with a collar around your neck, just like a little dog."

At first Kenneth thought that would be his only punishment, but he was completely wrong. Rich took the little boy's clothes off and dragged him to his room. Kenneth started screaming, knowing that he was about to be beaten like some criminal who had just broken out of prison. "Please!" the boy pleaded. "Please, don't beat me!"

In the background, little Danny started crying. Danny loved his brother so much that it made him cry whenever he saw Rich beating his brother. Even though Danny and Kenneth had different fathers, they were very close.

Rich was a very cruel person. To everyone who didn't have anything to do with him, he was the meanest you had ever seen. He beat the little boy so badly that, after awhile, the pain was gone; his body had shut down, and he'd moved past the physical pain.

Danny hated when this happened to Kenneth because he loved his big brother so much. He would cry when he heard his father say, "That little bastard, Kenneth, and his two half sisters are nothing of mine. As far as I'm concerned, they're scum just like their fathers."

Rich would turn his anger on the children's mom too. "Bitch," the man would yell, "if you weren't such a tramp, these little crumbs wouldn't have even been created! But a woman who likes to screw as much as you can't help the problems that she causes." After these words of sarcasm, Kenneth would hear a few smacks. And later, Rich would tell Kenneth's mom that the only kids he wanted in his house were the two kids that were his—Danny and Reggie. Saying this, he would leave and go get drunk at a local bar. Then he would wander off and be gone somewhere for a few days.

When Rich finally did come back, he would bring flowers for the strong, but weak with grief mother of the household. Anne would give him a faint smile, the sadness never leaving her eyes. Even though she loved him, a part of her probably hoped that whenever he went out he would never come back. But he had to return because, after lying with some whore for a few days, he missed abusing everyone at home.

Dinnertime rolled around, and Patty and Rita were helping their mother prepare the meal. Rich was already sitting at the head of the table, as if he were a king. He was a big shot in his mind, though no one else thought of him that way. The baby was in his own little chair, with his table, playing with his spoon. Little Reggie was always a happy baby, and to his great fortune, he wasn't old enough to detect the depressing feeling that had set over everyone in the household.

Danny walked into the dining room, and Kenneth slowly followed behind his little brother.

"Rich, what's the matter with Kenneth?" Anne wanted to know.

"He's not going to eat nothing for dinner," Rich snapped. "And if he's hungry, he can suck the marrow out of the bones that we leave when we finish. When he's done, he can go to his room, and I don't want him out till tomorrow night after I whip his little ass like I did tonight. You don't know what he did, do you, Anne?"

"No, what did he do?" Anne said softly, looking at her no-excuse-for-a-man husband.

"Why that little son of yours, he ruined our bedroom walls, drawing all over them with crayons and poured your perfume all over the room. Now, if he doesn't deserve the punishment he's getting, I just don't know what's wrong with anybody around here."

Rita giggled, but Patty didn't, as she, too, had been badly mistreated by Rich. Rita had just been lucky so far; Rich had hit her only a few times.

"Rich," Anne said, using a line she often tried, "I know Kenneth should be punished—I agree—but not the way you are going about it. You're showing more of the hate you have, as you say, to my son. And I don't like it."

"Shut up!" Rich growled. "I know what I'm doing. You don't know what the hell you're talking about, so let me do it my way, okay?"

Even though it wasn't okay, Anne put her head down, too hurt to fight. She wouldn't say anything more, so Rich had won again, like he always did.

After dinner was over, everyone left ready to go to bed or, for those who were allowed, to watch TV. When Rich wasn't there, everyone in the house would watch television and eat dessert together. The family could still do this when Rich was home, but nobody wanted to be around him if they could help it, so the kids generally made themselves scarce after dinner.

Tonight, Patty helped Anne wash dishes, and Kenneth went back to his room. Danny was sound asleep. Confused, Kenneth petted Tiger, who loved the boy very much. The cat would never forget the rainy day when he had been saved by his present master and faithful friend.

It was a star-gleaming, extra bright night, and Kenneth was looking out his window when he suddenly heard the door open. His heart jumped to his throat; he thought his stepfather had come back to whip him some more.

Instead, he heard his mother's voice. "Honey, I brought you some chicken. I wasn't that hungry, and Rich thought I threw it out, so hurry up and eat it before he comes in and sees you, because we'll both be in big trouble.

"Kenneth," she added after a moment, "I want to send you and your sisters away very soon. You have an uncle and aunt who are going to meet you very soon. They would like to adopt you, and you would become legally their son, with their last name.

"Your sisters will go to live with their real father," she explained. "I think you'll be very happy, once you leave here."

With that, Kenneth kissed his mother good night. While she was telling him her plans he'd finished up the meal that she'd snuck to him.

Wow, that might be really nice, he thought, imagining his aunt and uncle. *I'll call them Mommy and Daddy.* He decided he would really enjoy that. *And they'll love me.* He smiled.

*　　*　　*

The big day came when Kenneth was to meet his new parents—his future parents, that is.

"Look at that red-and-black car, Mommy."

Anne looked out the window. "Oh, yeah, that's your aunt and uncle," she told him.

The man and woman both got out of their car and walked toward the house. Smiles spread over their faces as they came inside to meet little Kenneth. Luckily, Rich was gone again, out on another of his few day sprees.

"Kenneth," Anne said, "this is your uncle Harold and your aunt Mary."

"Hi, Kenneth. How ya doin'?" Mary asked.

Kenneth looked up at the lady with the beautiful smile and said, "I'm doin' okay, Aunt Mary."

"Oh, he's something else, isn't he?" The man who was his uncle Harold, looked at Kenneth. Smiling, he added, "You need some meat on your bones, kid." Harold not knowing what type of food the little boy was eating, which was mostly the inside of the bones.

Kenneth enjoyed going out with Uncle Harold and Aunt Mary that day. Then the weekends he spent with them became more frequent. Soon, they decided to let him stay with them for a few weeks and see how that went.

Harold and Mary treated him really well. They took him to different places and bought him some clothes, as he really didn't have any. He often wore his sister's undershirts and other hand-me-down items. He basically was a little ragamuffin.

One day, Kenneth, Harold, and Mary were sitting at the table having dinner, and Uncle Harold said, "So, Kenneth, would you like to be my son?"

"Really?" Kenneth said. "That would be swell. Wow. You'll be my daddy, and Aunt Mary will be my mommy?"

"Yes, son, and we'll always do the best we can for you and teach you as much as possible about doing the right things in life," Harold said. "We'll ask your mother and see what she says, okay? Now let's go get some ice cream, and we'll have a good ride."

Harold and Mary spoke to Anne about adopting Kenneth, and Anne agreed. She had to look out for her son's well-being, and she determined that being away from Rich was in Kenneth's best interest. She wanted him to have a better life than the misery he was living in—a life away from such a hateful person.

So Kenneth kissed his mother good-bye.

"I'll always be in touch with you, son," she assured him. "Don't worry. And I'm always going to be your mother."

"Okay, Mommy. I love you," Kenneth said. "I'll see you soon."

"I will speak to you soon, son," his mother replied. "But I want you to get adjusted, and maybe if you don't see me for a while, it'll be easier. That way, you can get used to being with Uncle Harold and Aunt Mary, who will be your other mommy and daddy.

"And you do the best you can and listen to them, okay?" she added. "Be happy and have a good life. I love you, son."

"I love you too, Mommy," Kenneth told her. "Good-bye!"

*   *   *

Kenneth was adopted, and his new name was Kenneth Harold Thompson. That was some name, huh. Anyway, he enjoyed being with his new parents, Harold and Mary.

The trio would ride around a lot, often going upstate to Monticello to see Uncle Brian and his wife, Aunt Sarah, and Kenneth's cousins. They all had a good time on those visits. Kenneth loved to swim in Brian and Sarah's pool because there were frogs in it. The frogs would hop in and out of the pool, and everyone had a lot of fun.

Uncle Brian was one of Harold's brothers. His other two brothers were Uncle Sammy and Uncle Chris. Later in life, these four brothers would become for Kenneth—who had become KenBrownEagle—representations of the four elements of directions: east, west, north, and south. These were the eagles—the mighty ones, from the Powhatan Nation and also the Montauks.

The family had gotten their last name, Thompson, from a chieftain of the Powhatan tribe in Virginia. Black Feather had married an English woman whose last name was Thompson, and they had inherited her last name.

*   *   *

The first school that Kenneth went to was a parochial school called St. Peter and St. Paul in Jamaica, Queens. Everyone wore uniforms, and the teachers were nuns. You might think the nuns were really nice, but they would hit you hard if you did something wrong, with a paddle. Kenneth got paddled a lot. Kenneth wasn't very good in school. He used to play a lot.

After parochial school the family started building a house in Greenlawn, Long Island, and Kenneth changed schools. His new school was called Manor Plains.

While the house was being built, Harold, Mary, and Kenneth went to live with a new aunt and uncle. Aunt Loraine and Uncle Buster lived in Islip, Long Island, and Kenneth went to school there temporarily.

Behavior problems started to arise with little Kenneth at the Islip school. Kenneth didn't like being picked on, and he would stand on his own two feet in defense. When a kid at the school targeted him, hitting him and picking on him, Kenneth took matters into his own hands. He was being bullied.

One day Kenneth said to the kid, "Hey, say ah."

"What do you mean?" the kid asked.

"Look, just say ah. Let me just take your temperature."

"I'll play your stupid game this once if you give me your lunch," the kid replied.

Kenneth agreed, and the kid opened his mouth wide. "Ahhh."

At that instant, Kenneth broke the ice cream stick in the bully's throat. Now that was quite a violent response for a little child, or anyone.

*   *   *

A year went by, and by now Kenneth was in first grade, as he'd been held back, mostly because of behavior. He had been suspended for nearly a year because of the ice cream stick incident, and he didn't return to school in Islip. The house in Greenlawn was finished, and Kenneth would start a new life there. He felt that his behavior problems would go through more obstacles and that he would deal with other people's behavior.

Another problem Kenneth faced was Mary's drinking; she used to drink a lot of wine. During the daytime, early in the day, she was a nice person, and then at night, she was completely opposite—a regular Jekyll and Hyde. She would abuse Kenneth by making him perform tedious or degrading tasks. One time, on his birthday, she woke him up at three o'clock in the morning and made him scrub the floor in the bathroom by hand with a toothbrush. Her behavior toward him was really cruel, and Kenneth didn't need to face cruelty at home again. These incidents had a spiral effect, and Kenneth's behavior in school became more and more unbalanced; he was either a class clown or very disruptive. And sometimes, he didn't go to school at all.

His truancy eventually got him in some deep trouble at home. One day, he sneaked back into the house after Mary had gone to work—as he'd done for the past three days. He planned to watch television all day again. He'd been having a great time acting like he'd gone to school. He would take his school clothes off, put his play clothes on and sit and watch shows like *The Three Stooges* and *The Merry Mailman* all day. He'd been using the key, which he had because Mary wouldn't be home by the time he got home from school. She was an excellent tailor, and her job as a seamstress for a very well-known store would get her home later than when Kenneth would get home from school.

On this particular day, Kenneth had settled in for a day of television when, suddenly, he was surprised by the sound of a car door closing. It was Mary. She wasn't driving at the time and had taken a cab back home. She rushed into the house. Kenneth ran and hid under the bed. Mary looked in his closet and saw that his school clothes—the ones she was sure he had been wearing—were hung up. It didn't take much for her to discover his hiding spot.

She went straight to the bed, dragged him out, and started hitting him. "Wait till your father comes home," she told him. "He is going to beat you with his belt."

Kenneth did get a beating that night, and he would never forget that episode; it would stay with him in both his younger years and into his adult life.

One of Kenneth's fears was giving his parents a bad report card, as they were very strict. So when he received one, he forged their signatures on the report card and turned it in to the teacher. The signature didn't match those on the previous better report cards that his parents had actually signed, and the teacher called his parents. He got two beatings—one from each parent. He was in trouble for a long time after thatThe only problem that Kenneth had with his new parents as a couple was that, early in the relationship, Mary and Harold argued a lot. Mary's alcohol-induced dual personality obviously played a role. She would scream Kenneth's father all the time, and she was very mean to Kenneth. She gave Kenneth a beating one time because he killed a moth that was in his bed. He was always being sent to his room for the slightest things as so-called punishment.

With all this time in his room, Kenneth read a lot. He enjoyed the other worlds of fantasy he found in books. Mythology was his favorite. He also enjoyed biographies about presidents, various heroes, and people of importance.

Kenneth learned a lot in history class, his favorite subject. He wasn't at all good at math. In Science he was always getting Fs. He liked gym and was very accomplished in different types of sports.

He used to play a lot outside and was very mischievous. For instance, he got a kick out of standing under the girls when they were going up the steps to the slide so he could look under their dresses—he'd do mischievous things, things that most boys did then.

He was always in detention after school and would have to write, "I will not do this, and I will not do that." Whatever the reason for his being held after school, the teacher would decide the punishment.

Sometimes he would get up from his seat in class, walk out, and go somewhere. He didn't want to be at school. Well this started to be a problem for the officials, and that's when Kenneth first experienced where such problems might lead. One day, the school nurse called him to the office. He thought he just had to see her about something and was surprised when a truancy officer met him in the office.

"Kenneth, you'd better come with me," the officer said. "I'm going to take you to a type of youth house, a facility for truant children and minors who have committed other offenses." The officer explained that Kenneth was what they called a "wayward minor"; in other words, he was, to the authorities, a juvenile delinquent.

That time turned out to be just a scare. The truancy officer didn't really take Kenneth away, but the threat—the idea that he would be going somewhere—made him nervous enough.

Kenneth was really a very good child. He just liked to play a lot. As a young boy, he liked to get into mischief. And, basically, he just didn't like to go to school. His parents, though, were very strict.

Harold was a teacher at Benjamin Franklin High School in Manhattan, New York. There, he had to deal with students and staff from extremely varied walks of life and all types of personalities, and he actually got along with and was respected by everybody there. All the students loved him. They called him either Mr. Thompson or Mr. Harold, but they all respected him. And that was because he gave them respect. And that was how Kenneth grew up—he respected people and expected the same in return.

One of Kenneth's favorite things to do in the wintortime was to go on toboggan rides at the nearby sandpits. He and his friends, joined by kids from other adjoining neighborhoods would construct trails through the sandpits and in the woods. The combination was some ride.

A funny thing used to happen when Kenneth would go to the sandpit to play. The land across the street was an animal reserve, and a crow who resided there liked to tease Kenneth. The crow didn't hurt him, but whenever the crow knew that Kenneth was in the area, walking on his way to play, it would startle him, swooping down and snatching the boy's hat from his head.

Kenneth and his parents were very involved with church. He was baptized and was given communion as an Episcopalian. Harold was in the choir, and Kenneth was an acolyte. His participation in church was a wonderful experience. The family enjoyed going to midnight Mass on Christmas Eve. For Kenneth, that was a glorious experience; he would get to stay up late, and he would also be able to be an altar boy. He thoroughly enjoyed those Christmas Eves.

The sport Kenneth wasn't good at was baseball. He wanted and tried to be good at it, but he just wasn't. He was in Little League and sure looked good in his uniform, and he liked wearing it. He was able to ride his bicycle to the field where his team practiced and had their games. The baseball park wasn't very far from home either. Unfortunately, though, he wasn't the best player.

Kenneth was good at football, wrestling, gymnastics, and track. He was especially good in track, like his father, Harold. He raced the 50-yard dash and the 100-yard dash and also liked the running broad jump. He also excelled when it came to taking the marine test in school. He came in second in junior high school. Another kid at school used to beat him in everything they did.

Things between Harold and Mary weren't getting any better. They argued all the time, and the constant turmoil made Kenneth rebellious in different ways. For example, he was at the age now where his friends and schoolmates would throw parties occasionally, and Kenneth was never allowed to go. So he would just sneak out his window and go to the party. He'd make his bed up like somebody was in it, and after he'd left the party, he would sneak in the window and go to bed. That was pretty clever for a twelve-year-old.

He also started drinking when he went to parties and experienced for the first time what it was to get drunk. One time, he found himself flying off the porch at a girl's home. She was having a party, and Kenneth got drunk and started cursing and yelling. Somebody ended up picking him up and throwing him off the front porch. He did apologize to the whole family later, but that was an early sign that Kenneth wasn't really a drinker.

*   *   *

"Kenneth, your grandma's on the phone!"

Oh, wow, he thought. *Maybe I'm going to be able to visit again for the holidays.* Kenneth loved his grandma.

"Hi, Kenneth, would you like to come and visit again after Christmas day and stay with us for a week? You can go to Uncle Alonso and Aunt Helen's house for a few days also."

"Oh, I'd love that, Grandma," Kenneth assured her. "I always love to come and visit you."

"Okay we'll come and see you at Christmas, so we can pick you up and bring you back home with us."

"Oh wow, thanks, Grandma."

"I love you," she said.

"I love you, Grandma."

Kenneth's grandma, Frances Babcock, was a wonderful, church-going lady. She was always very kind. The only time that

Kenneth ever saw her get upset was when her two daughters—Mary and Helen—would argue. On almost every occasion when the two argued, they would have been drinking, and Grandma Frances would cry. Often, when the whole family was visiting, they would end up going back home to Greenlawn early because Harold had had enough until the next holiday.

The arguments, his grandma's sadness, and leaving early used to make Kenneth sad. It seemed like he had come into this world surrounded by negativity, arguing, and abuse. Even after going to live with his new parents, this negativity was still present. He began to wonder, *Where are the nice people?*. His grandma, of course, was nice, as were his aunt Helen and uncle Alonzo. He always had a great time with them, but he didn't see them much.

His mother used to call sometimes, but Mary would tell her that he wasn't there.

Kenneth's solo visits to see Grandma Frances and Aunt Helen and Uncle Alonso's was wonderful. When he was staying at his grandma's for a few days, they would do activities like going to the movies and then to a restaurant to have hamburgers with lettuce and tomatoes and French fries and Kenneth's favorite, root beer. At the movies, Neccos were his favorite candy.

Kenneth also used to love watching television. He could sit or lie down and watch TV for hours. Watching the tube was a sort of escape; he would get away from other thoughts—the thoughts that had scarred him a little. Sometimes, he would thinks of Rich beating him and taking him to the beach and forcing him go into the water so the salt water would burn his wounds. That particular beating also left a scar on Kenneth's private area.

Another reason he enjoyed spending time with his aunt and uncle was their playfulness. They would listen to music and dance in front of Kenneth and laugh and have a good time. Uncle Alonso was a cheerful fella. He would say, "Hey! Whadda you say? How ya doin', kiddo?"

Kenneth also had a girlfriend in that neighborhood. Her name was Cheryl, and she was very pretty. That was one of his first experiences of having strong feelings for a member of the opposite sex. Kissing and sharing strong feelings for one another was as far as his and Cheryl's relationship went. She said that she was seeing this other guy. But whenever Kenneth went to visit, she would see him also. Kenneth couldn't complain about that.

The other thing Kenneth liked doing was drinking Ripple—the equivalent back then of today's wine coolers. Ripple, though, was a lot stronger; or maybe Kenneth thought that because he was only a kid. Ripple was thirty-two cents a pint, and it came in a variety of flavors, including grape, cherry, and pineapple. Kenneth used to get fired up on that; that was one of his early obstacles. Another was smoking cigarettes, which he started just to be cool.

He first tried cigarettes at the age of ten. He took a few of Mary's cigarettes. She smoked non-filter Philip Morris, and they were strong. He thought he was getting away with smoking in the bathroom and that no one would know if he opened the window. But of course his parents smelled the smoke, and he got punished for that. He would be sent to his room again, where he would listen to his transistor radio or read.

One of his favorite radio stations was WWRL, and the "Swingin' Soiree" with Murray the K and Cousin Brucie. The station played a lot of nice hits. At the time, the Beatles were new and popular, as were the Rolling Stones, Herman and the Hermits, the Marvelettes, Temptations, the Four Tops, and on and on. Kenneth liked any group that sounded good. He also had his own record player that played 45s and 33 and 1/2s and a record collection, gifts from his grandmother and aunt and uncle.

Holidays with Grandma Frances and Aunt Helen and Uncle Alonso went quickly, and then Kenneth would be back home with his parents. He loved his father dearly, but he didn't like the abuse he was getting from Mary. She would be coldhearted one moment and very nice the next. Her split personality was sad; either you loved her or you didn't like her, but you couldn't just feel one feeling about her.

Mary did a lot of nice things too. She made a lot of Kenneth's clothes. She was also the one who'd had the idea about the YMCA to hopefully help his behavior. She always wanted Kenneth to be good and dress nicely. She wanted him to be polite and raised him to respect others. She just had the alcohol addiction, which changed her whole personality and interrupted her balance.

As Kenneth grew older and Mary wasn't getting any better, he started to run away from home.

Harold and Mary finally split up and got divorced. Mary said that Harold had gone to be with an old girlfriend of his. This left Kenneth at home with Mary, who was an angel in the day and a devil at night. What a frightening thing for a child to go through.

He rebelled and ran away and started getting picked up by the police and taken to the Hauppauge shelter for boys and girls. The shelter had rooms that were just like adult jail cells, with a little window on the door and strong mesh on the windows that looked outside. The only difference between adult jails and the shelter was the ages of the inmates. The counselors weren't the nicest either. One of the staff used to enjoy cooking steak while everyone was locked in his or her room, teasing the boys and girls with the smell.

The girls and boys would communicate with each other by sneaking notes. They would pass the word to one another in the cafeteria or back and forth during school, telling each other where a message was in a certain book in a certain classroom that they would all eventually go to. That was fun!

What wasn't fun was whenever someone got in trouble; he or she would be locked in his or her room for twenty-four or forty-eight hours, not allowed to come out at all.

After a few months at the shelter, Kenneth would be let out. He'd go back to school, but he'd eventually run away again, and the cycle would start all over. He'd get locked up, and he was on his way to really becoming a juvenile delinquent. He despised Mary and missed his father. So after this rebelling had gone on for some time, the authorities transferred him from Hauppauge shelter to a place called Berkshire Farm for Boys in upstate New York. He spent eighteen months at Berkshire.

Berkshire Farms was really a nice place; it was away from everything Kenneth was going through, which he enjoyed a lot. He also enjoyed being upstate—the fresh air and mingling with different children from all walks of life. When they were good, the Berkshire boys were allowed to visit their family for a few days on passes, and Kenneth liked visiting his grandma.

They were also allowed to go to dances as a reward for good behavior. The facility would arrange dances with places like Hudson Training School for Girls and Wineskill, which was in Troy, New York. The boys and girls weren't allowed to touch each other, except when they were dancing. They could also slow dance, which was very nice and as intimate as you could get. Then when they returned to Berkshire, the boys were able to write letters to someone they'd met at the dance. That's when Kenneth started to enjoy creative writing; he'd use rhymes, for example, writing lines to the girls like, "As I sit on this wheel of action, I'm getting a little satisfaction, thinking of you."

Berkshire Farms also used to hold talent shows. Kenneth liked to play Smokey in the group Smokey Robinson and the Miracles.

They boys lived in cottages. They went to school and on field trips, in addition to the dances. The boys were divided into five groups, according to their behavior. Five was the highest-ranking group, and those in that group got all the extra privileges. Kenneth was usually in group two. After a year and a half, his behavior started to improve, and he did get as far as four. Still, he did get himself into a little mischief from time to time.

He became a pool shark and would win a lot of the other boys' commissary tender for which they could buy things from the store. There was a store there on the grounds and you were able to buy cigarettes or candy. He would win a lot of cigarettes or the other boy's clothing, their vines. That's what they called clothes back in the 1960s—when you were "vinin'," your apparel was smooth and you were cool. Kenneth had some cool green pants, and a pair of gold and silver sharkskins. Some of his pants were gifts from his buddies when they left to go home or, for those who were going further in the penitentiary system, to prison. Considered adults at the age of sixteen, the boys who had committed serious crimes would go into the court system, which would order the remainder of their sentences to be carried out in an adult facility. Berkshire was a holding spot for juveniles under the age of sixteen. The next stop for everyone was either home or prison

Another thing that got Kenneth in trouble was his general disdain for too much authority. And he didn't like a lot of hard work. He worked in the kitchen washing dishes, and one day, he got so sick of so many dishes that he started flinging them up in the woods. The kitchen staff eventually noticed a decrease in the number of dishes and figured out what he was doing. And that was the end of that job.

Mary kept in touch with Kenneth while he was upstate and visited one time with a new friend of hers—a gentleman named J. D., short for John Duncan. Her new man seemed to be a nice guy. J. D. was a little older than Mary, but he was a pleasant person. He told Kenneth that he would be the best friend Kenneth could have, if he could. That was nice to hear. In other words, Kenneth was going to get another chance to stay in Greenlawn, at home with Mary. At first, she wasn't going to let him come back. But she decided to give him a chance to change his juvenile delinquency; she would allow him to visit first and play it by ear.

A few of the visits worked out pretty well, but then they didn't. J. D. was also a drinker, and he would get a little nasty. One of his comments to Kenneth was, "You know what? I'm from the city in Harlem, and I don't play." He flicked out a switchblade and showed it to Kenneth. "I'll cut somebody up in a minute if they mess with me," he said.

After that, Kenneth didn't really like J. D. anymore. The incident ended that relationship. So that was it for living in Greenlawn.

Kenneth decided that he would like to live with his father again and with Harold's new wife, LaFawn. LaFawn was a nice person. Before making the move, he visited the couple so that he could meet her. She was warm and caring. She also cooked well. "Maybe you can live with us eventually," she told Kenneth.

She said *eventually* because, after reform school, Kenneth would have his freedom, but he would have to stay in a place called a halfway house, where other teenagers lived while looking for jobs or attending school. Everyone in the house had chores. The teens ate and lived there. Those who had family got weekend passes to visit them.

Visits were really nice, and Kenneth enjoyed his new future mother because she was so nice to him. Harold was happy too. Harold and LaFawn lived in Manhattan, between Broadway and Riverside Drive on 139th Street. Up on Broadway and Riverside Drive, you'd find a variety of different cultures, and then on Amsterdam Avenue, an entirely different set of cultures flourished, and Kenneth was able to watch and interact with people from many different walks of life.

Kenneth also enjoyed staying at the halfway house; the neighborhood was nice as far as he was concerned. He met one of his new girlfriends, and they had a relationship, only she had another boyfriend at the same time. That relationship didn't last too long.

Kenneth ended up going to another halfway house in the Bronx off of Gun Hill on 215th Street. He attended a high school called Evander Childs. He liked where he lived at first, and school was pretty good. Everybody was vinin', and everybody was into dope (heroin). Back then, you could get a "deuce"—a two-dollar bag. Before long, Kenneth started experimenting with the stuff. It was the wrong move, but he didn't realize it at the time. His heroin use started with sniffing. He would get really high and start nodding and hardly ever went to classes. Then he moved to skin poppin' in a muscle, usually in the back of the arm, using a hypodermic needle and syringe to inject the drug. He was never in school anymore. He and the boys would hang out outside of school looking sharp, clean as the board of health, but also in love with that heroin.

After awhile, things started really getting out of hand. Kenneth started to sell a little bit for other dealers who were better known in the area. The main thing in those days was listening to good music, rapping to the ladies, vinin', and having a dollar in your pocket, as well as a little bit of heroin or cocaine. On the weekends, everyone would go to places like the Audubon Ballroom or the Manhattan Center.

The halfway house and the counselors there weren't working out for Kenneth anymore, so he asked his father and stepmother if he could live with them and still go to Evander Childs. He would commute on the train. They spoke to the authorities at the halfway house, and everyone agreed this would be the best situation.

Kenneth decided he was going to have a different life and do better, but that didn't work out so well. One time, the guidance counselor called his parents and said that he looked like a dope dealer. The counselor warned them that, if Kenneth wasn't careful this would become a problem and he would end up signing out of school or going to jail if he got busted.

His stepmother, Fawn, used to take him to a place called Caesar's Alley hat sell's sweaters and other clothes. They would sell sweaters that were similar to those sold in stores downtown, only with a different label and less expensive. Fawn would spoil him a lot with clothes. In addition to his alpacas and salt-and-pepper silk pants, Kenneth had nice shoes. He liked Playboy shoes and alligator, lizard, and snakeskin shoes in all colors. The shoes were part of the vining and made the whole outfit complete; he wore a different outfit from top to bottom every day.

He would always remember one outfit that he wore to the Audubon Ballroom to see the Emotions and some other R & B soul and Latin groups. His mom had bought him this alpaca sweater that was also leather and Persian lamb; it was black, red, and white, and it was sharp. You couldn't tell Kenneth anything, and he had some dope with him too. When he went to the Audubon, he really didn't know much about the show because he was doped up and trying to be a big shot, selling deuces.

The music in the Evander Childs' days in the late 1960s was really good. Groups like Junior Walker and the All-Stars were really jammin'—they called it "fly." That music was the serious fly joint.

James Brown had a new side all the time. And there were good Latin groups, including Willie Colon and Ray Pacheco. Kenneth and his friends enjoyed all types of music from different cultures and nationalities. Kenneth always liked music.

As far as the girlfriend situation, Kenneth always had a nice girlfriend at first, and most of the time, the relationships changed due to circumstances. For example, he went with one young lady named Sonia, who was really beautiful. But the only way that Kenneth could see Sonia was if he sneaked into her parents' house. She lived downstairs, and he almost got caught sneaking out one time. That had to stop, and she quit him also because he was on drugs. Oddly, about a year later, he would see Sonia on drugs. Wasn't that sad?

Kenneth's drug problem was becoming a big problem. He had really become addicted. He even, one time, took a ring that his parents had given him and pawned it at a pawnshop in downtown Manhattan for drugs. His parents knew something was wrong then. Another time, he was sitting at the foot of the bed in his parents' room, supposedly watching television, and he started nodding.

His father yelled at him, "Kenneth, what are you doing? Are you on something?"

Kenneth would just sit there and lie and nod. His father would get very angry, and his stepmother was disappointed in him. The skin popping escalated to mainlining. Mainlining, or "booting" was when you boiled the heroin or cocaine in a spoon with a piece of cotton and then drew it out with a syringe and a needle; tying your arm up, you would inject the needle directly into your vein. You would wait for a boot, a hit, and then boot again and get immediate results.

Kenneth's habit was starting to become a little expensive, as, without him fully realizing what was happening, his weekend highs were turning into more than the weekend, and he was developing both a physical and mental need for the heroin. That was his drug of choice; the cocaine would come later.

Once again, he wasn't doing well in school. Kenneth was also having a little bit of a communication problem with his parents. For one thing, they knew what he was doing. He thought he was always slick, but they were two steps ahead of him. Once, he had wrapped up his syringe—his "works"—like a Christmas present and put it in his coat pocket, and his father found it. Harold confronted him with it. "Kenneth, what's this?" he asked.

Kenneth was speechless

"I knew you were on that dope," his father said.

He looked at his father, prepared to deny it, but his father said, "Don't you even try it."

Fawn started to pay attention to what was going on with Kenneth. She would call up his school to make sure that he attended all his classes. She discovered that, while he went to school a lot of times, more often, he didn't go at all.

The problems at home escalated to a point where, home life was a living nightmare for both Kenneth and his parents. As Kenneth's heroin addiction escalated, so did his desperateness to get money to buy more heroin. It was very hard for Kenneth to look normal in appearance to other people, and his secret addiction only made things worse His life was becoming very cloudy and dark. The more he got involved in the drugs, the more problems came his way. Kenneth loved God and knew that, for some reason, he would always be guided by a force that would reprimand him when he was wrong. And right now he was being reprimanded because he was definitely living his life the wrong way. So, the problems he endured were a result of cause and effect; what he was doing was coming back to him. His Karma—he could call it a lot of different things—wasn't good.

Kenneth felt a spiritual spirit in his life, but he didn't yet know what it was. Hai hayhis, sound, for example—a positive sound that was part of Native American tradition—would come to Kenneth later. He always liked to discover whatever he could about the unknown, and his reading earlier in life—the different adventures and fantasies in history and mythology—remained with him. So his mind wandered a lot. Kenneth used to ask himself why, if he loved God and knew that God was there to guide him through these things of darkness? Did the Great Spirit want Kenneth to know about this side of life? Was there value in experiencing these storms that he as an individual and everyone in the world goes through? Perhaps he needed to learn about cause and effects. But he really didn't have any answers yet.

One day, Kenneth started thinking about robbing a neighbor of his parents. He climbed from his parents' terrace on the thirteenth floor across to her terrace next door. Once in the woman's apartment, he took her fur coats. In a panic, he quickly left her home and ran down the hallway through a door in the staircase. He ran down to another staircase and hid the coats behind a door that stayed open, hiding them.

When the neighbor discovered that she had been robbed, a big commotion ensued. Kenneth's parents were suspicious, but they didn't say. Rather, they focused their attention on their son.

Luckily Kenneth's parents looked in the building and found the neighbor's fur coats behind the door on the other staircase. They knew Kenneth was responsible but couldn't prove it because he wouldn't confess.

Kenneth got himself a little hustle around the neighborhood, shining shoes on 137th Street and Broadway. His friend, Lefty introduced him to the shoe shining business. Lefty's spot was right outside the train station entrance. Lefty was also involved in heroin.

Often, the two would get high together, and Lefty would share his shining business. It was frequently quite busy at the stop, and a lot of days, they would make a hundred bucks. Sometimes the take was a little less, but they made money every day, and that was their spot, their corner.

They also had another friend, Poet. Poet was always clean as the board of health, but he sold dope.

Kenneth pretended that things with his parents were going well; he wasn't having any problems as far as finances were concerned. He was hustling.

He also had a girlfriend, the daughter of a work friend of Fawn's. Tina Marie was a good friend, and she and Kenneth had a sexual relationship in the beginning of their relationship. The relationship didn't last long because Tina Marie moved and because of Kenneth's continued involvement in the drug life. But they did have a nice relationship for the brief time that it lasted. Tina Marie used to love to sing "Pillow Talk" by Sylvia Robinson. It was a very sensual song, and Tina Marie sang it very sensually.

School was finished for Kenneth once he'd reached the tenth grade. He was asked to sign himself out of school; he was given that ultimatum that the guidance counselor had told his parents about earlier that year—either he would sign himself out of school or be prosecuted for something and go to jail. He signed himself out.

And then his parents gave him another ultimatum. He was to either find a job or go into the service. At the time, the United States was involved with the Vietnam War, and he definitely didn't want to go to Vietnam. In addition, he was getting into more and more trouble.

Finally, he pulled the straw that broke the camel's back. One day his inquisitive, wandering mind took him into his parent's closet, where he discovered a metal box. He opened it, and to his surprise, they kept jewels in the box; they even had insurance papers to go along with the jewels.

Suddenly he heard someone come to the door and open it. He panicked and put the box under the bed instead of back in the closet.

When his father discovered what had happened, he picked Kenneth up and threw him across the room. "I should throw you right off the terrace," he yelled. "You don't live here anymore. Get out! You're on your own now. Get out!"

*   *   *

And Kenneth was out there in the world by himself. He stayed in the neighborhood for awhile shining shoes, hanging out with Lefty and Poet. The trio would wheel and deal. Once in a while, Poet would give him a little package, or he would wander downtown and see what was going on down there.

Things grew increasingly crazy. Down on the lower east side—with Avenues A, B, C, and D, people used to call it the alphabet jungle (and probably still do)—Kenneth learned a lot about the drug and crime worlds. Soon, Kenneth rarely went uptown anymore. One time, he passed his father, and his father acted like he didn't even see him. He was so ashamed and disappointed.

Living downtown, Kenneth often just lived in the street. As long as he had his dope, that was fine with him; he always had a place to crash—a shooting gallery or an abandoned building or a bathroom in the hallway, but somewhere. When he was awake, he would be in the street hustling.

In the late '60s and early '70s, Kenneth's generation took a lot of acid, a nickname for LSD. One of his hustles was robbing somebody named Sunshine Jack. Sunshine Jack sold Orange Sunshine, Yellow

Sunshine, and tabs. One day, Kenneth gave him a choice that he couldn't refuse.First he showed him that he had a weapon and a voice and appearance of intimidation "I want all the tabs that you have on you," Kenneth told him. "You can keep some of the money because I'm not a creep, but every time I see you, whatever tabs you got on you, turn them right over. Don't ask anything. You know what time it is. You'll know exactly what I want."

For another hustle, Kenneth would bring somebody who was interested in buying drugs to his part of town, which was in the jungle along one of the avenues, and rob them. Or he'd go to Washington Square Park, depending on what day or time it was, when most of the police weren't around. Often, he could panhandle a few hundred bucks in a day.

One night he must have gotten a little greedy, since things were going so well with the robberies and he had money in his pocket. He was going back and forth between getting high and going out there to hustle, pulling a little con here and there, or pull off a robbery. He never physically harmed anyone though. At times, he would escort a person part of the way to wherever they were going next. He would even give them a few bucks back. On this particular night, he ran into two guys who were going into a building, and he robbed them.

When Kenneth ran out of the building and dashed around the corner, he all of a sudden saw car lights and sirens coming from every direction. A car screeched to a stop, and two police officers jumped out. Other cops were running on foot from around the block; the officers smashed him against the wall. He was arrested, charged with robbery, and taken to jail.

The robbery victims went to court every single time that Kenneth had to appear at 100 Centre Street in Manhattan to face that charge. After being sentenced, Kenneth was incarcerated at Rikers Island in

East Elmhurst, Queens. The judge gave him one to three years; he would serve no less than one year and no more than three.

Unfortunately, every time he went in front of the parole board, he didn't make parole. Because of his behavior, the board would tell him to come back in nine months.

At Rikers Island, aka "the Rock," you had to be down when any static jumped off. Kenneth was in trouble all the time. The guards would put him in the Bing, which was jail in a jail, or solitary confinement, where he would be on close watch. They called it segregation. The inmates didn't go anywhere. They were just in another world.

Finally, Kenneth started to behave, got a job, and finished up his time. His parents visited him twice, and they were really sad to see him in this situation. But this, again, was an experience that Kenneth had to learn from—another storm he had to go through.

At the end of his bid, during his final year, Kenneth got a good job as the co-captain in the receiving room, earning either fifteen, eighteen and when he bacame the captain twenty-two dollars a week, which was good pay in jail in the early '70s. He also bought cash from people who were coming in off the street and were sick for the need of dope. He would buy their sneakers if they were new and give them cigarettes or cookies to help their sickness feel a little better.

Everything worked out, and Kenneth had finally done his entire thirty-six months. At the time, he was one of the oldest inmates on the Rock. Discharge day came, and Kenneth had a little money on him. The guards in administrationgave you money when you left, and he had earned some money when he was working in the receiving room. He still didn't return to live with his parents, though. Instead, he went back to his old stomping grounds, the lower east side, where he had gone through that drama with the robbery that had gotten him the three years due to his drug addiction.

Things on the lower east side didn't work out; he started shooting drugs again and started getting arrested again and again. He only did short bids—which the inmates called "skid bids"—that lasted from ninety days to six months.

After a few skid bids, Kenneth started to wise up and got a job. That's when he met a wonderful young woman named Carmen. Carmen was so beautiful. They met when he was standing on the corner of 47th and Broadway in midtown Manhattan. Dressed in a nice, three-piece suit and carrying an attaché case, he was selling office equipment.

She walked by him, and without thinking, he called to her, "Where are you going?"

"None of your business," she retorted. "What the heck are you worrying about where I'm going for?"

"I just wanted to know because I'd like to know you," he replied.

"I'm going right over here." She pointed a few buildings away. "I'm finishing up my break "

"What do you do?" he asked.

"I'm a dancer," she told him.

"Oh," he stuttered. "Oh you mean one of those, uh . . ."

"Yeah," she said. "I'm one of those topless dancers. I do all right for myself too. You got a problem with that?"

"No. No," he said quickly.

"Why don't you come and check out the show?" she suggested.

"Oh," he replied. "Oh. Okay"

He followed her inside. After a few minutes, she started to dance on the bar and stage. Other girls were dancing too, and this was a new experience for Kenneth, a new adventure.

Half West Indian, half Dominican, Carmen was beautiful, and Carmen was a beautiful name too. Wow he was in love. And she liked him too. Carmen was tough and feisty, which he didn't mind; that was adventurous.

He was a Sagittarius, and she was a Leo, and they got along. Occasionally, though, the relationship got a little out of hand, especially when Carmen would start drinking and taking downers. She liked to take Tuinals, and once again, Kenneth was dealing with a Jekyll and Hyde personality change. He thought of Mary, but this was a different type of a person, a different personality, and a different time in life. Only the root of the problem was the same.

Kenneth also had his own problems. He wasn't taking heroin anymore. He'd stopped after he'd been in and out of jail a few times and had gotten on the methadone program. So he was taking 80 milligrams of methadone every day.

Carmen was on the pills and the booze and dancing, and he was on the methadone and working two jobs. He was a salesman, during the day, and at night, he worked at a place called Orange Julius in Times Square. He was an assistant manager until he was fired for knocking somebody out who didn't pay, an offense he admitted to. This guy had come into the store and ordered food and some drinks. After he'd eaten everything, he left the store without paying. So Kenneth had chased him right to the middle of Times Square and knocked him right out before returning to the store.

It was just as well that he had got fired, because, even though he was in the right, it was a dangerous shift that he was working, and who knows what would have happened if he had stayed there. In addition, the manager had been trying to give him more responsibilities, including handling money in the safe, which wasn't very comfortable.

PART TWO

THIS AND THAT

Kenneth would never forget his introduction to an organization called Teen Challenge. That introduction took place some years back, when he was addicted to heroin. He had gone into an apartment building that had bathrooms in the hallways and had shot his dose of heroin. The dosage might have been a little stronger this time, because he'd ended up overdosing in the bathroom.

After some time, he'd come to and staggered out into the street, where he'd fallen out again. What he remembered was people stepping over him, as if he was a puddle or a piece of garbage, or nothing. Of the many people walking through the night, not knowing if he was dead or alive, no one would help him.

Then, if one believes in angels, some young people came to his aid. They got him up and walked him around to get him out of the overdose. Then they took him to a meeting that was being held in a storefront by a group called Teen Challenge. Kenneth slowly started to come out of the overdose; during the majority of the meeting he had been in and out of a deep nod and hadn't been aware of what anyone was saying. The group was trying to convince him that he needed help. They wanted to take him to Teen Challenge's house in Brooklyn, where he would be well taken care of. The Teen Challenge members told him that nuns were in charge of the house and he would be okay.

Kenneth knew that going with them would be good; he would really appreciate their help. So the teens took him to Brooklyn that night, and the nuns welcomed him. They gave him some nightclothes, and washed the clothes he was wearing, which hadn't been washed in days. As a homeless junkie, he wasn't thinking about washing clothes; he was thinking about getting a fix.

The nuns at the Teen Challenge house were very spiritual and prayed all night by the bed Kenneth was laying on. They prayed and prayed for hours, and he felt comfortable and safe. He was coming down off his last fix and was getting sick; in need of more, he was having the sweats and feeling really terrible.

So, unfortunately, he wanted to leave the next morning. He thanked the nuns for their help and their prayers. He got his clothes and went back out into the street because he really wanted some more dope, even though they had helped him.

And Kenneth would never forget the spiritual love the nuns at the house gave him. To this day, if he sees anyone from Teen Challenge, which is still in existence, he immediately gives them a donation. Through the group, people from the inner city could get help quickly through spiritual prayer and enlightenment; through the group's help, people had a chance to try and get off drugs.

Kenneth also read a book while he spent that night with Teen Challenge and the nuns. *The Cross and the Switchblade* was about the founder of Teen Challenge, who originally was a drug addict and was in a gang. But this man spiritually saw the Lord, and he changed over to the light side. He experienced moving through the darkness into the light. And that's what Kenneth has been doing for all these years—and in other lifetimes. (Kenneth would eventually study certain philosophies that involved reincarnation and his Native American ancestry and would come to a strong belief in reincarnation.)

Another thing Kenneth would always remember was the good advice that his father always gave him. Harold had taught him to be good and do for others and to be a balanced individual and spirit—to be a part of the world with a purpose and not just to take up space. His father really couldn't stand people who took up space. Harold instilled in Kenneth a desire for learning and for wisdom, and he gave his son love and always wanted him to do well in life. Kenneth would often recall his father's words or reflect on the time Harold put the word "THINK" on his wall, instead of pictures. Harold was a scholar, a man of unbelievable intelligence w a wonderful aura andheart, who cared for and loved to help others in need, mainly through teaching and guiding.

These were some of the things that Kenneth thought about when he was walking the different streets, day and night, feeling like he was the only one in the world facing this particular situation—the only drug addict out there. But millions of other people were in the same position or worse. This just happened to be his path in this life.

It would become crystal clear, though that, if it wasn't for the Lord, Kenneth wouldn't have survived. He always knew that God was with him, and he never debated with anyone about his or her thoughts or views. He knew what was in his heart. Even though he was going through a lot of darkness, he knew that God was there and was going to guide him through it. Often, he felt that God wanted him to know these things about life. As far as Kenneth was concerned, there was no other like the almighty God. He never put anyone down for their thoughts on religion or politics, even though he wasn't interested in politics.

The thing that disturbed him was that politics—the government in this country—was what had oppressed his people, the Native Americans. However, he forgave the government its mistakes and carries no hatred in his heart; he won't forget the past, but he's not the judge. The mistreatment of Native Americans was part of history, and people were supposed to be all in this together—united, as a people, no matter their color, their race or religion, or their nationality.

Kenneth would come to realize that we're all in this together. We're all God's people. Kenneth knew he wasn't perfect, far from it, but he wasn't bad either. And he was trying to find out different secrets of life. He was struggling to determine whether he wanted a happy life, a good future and good Karma.

Haaiiyay. Haaiiyayayay. Haaiiyay. Haaiiyayay—those were chants of *peace*. Kenneth was always proud of his heritage. On his mother's side, Kenneth was Creek, Scottish, and Black. The Creek Native Americans were and are in Alabama. His thoughts went back in time, way back, and he channeled the spirit of his great-great-great-great-grandfather, Osceola. Osceola led the second Seminole War. But before that, when Osceola was young, he and his mother were Creek. She married a man with the last name Powell, so Osceola's first name was William Powell. During a war in Alabama between the Red sticks and the White sticks, his mother and little William fled to Florida and joined up with the Seminole, who were related to the Creek.

As he grew older, Kenneth's relative got the name Osceola. One day, he and his friends were drinking a black liquid that made him make a noise that sounded like *asi yaholi*. Though *asi* couldn't be translated, it may have come from the Creek word *assi*, a black drink brewed from the leaves of the holly, *ilex vomitoria*, and prepared for annual ceremonies. The element *yaholi* may refer to the "yahola cry," a call to a Creek deity given when the black drink was served and at other times during the ceremony. The current simplified translation is Black Drink Singer. Osceola was proud of his people and would do anything for them. He was a very good man, even to his enemies. But he would defend his people to the fullest.

Osceola led the second Seminole War and ran the soldiers all through the swamps and everglades, which he and his warriors knew well. One day, the soldiers at Fort Moultrie in South Carolina summoned Osceola to talk peace with them. When Osceola and the warriors who were left with him arrived at the fort, they were placed under arrest. Deceived and tricked, the men were imprisoned.

Kenneth's great ancestor eventually passed away in prison. Records say that he died of malaria, but who really knows how he died?

After Osceola's death, his physician decapitated him and placed his head displayed in his drugstore window, with a sign that read, "This is the head of the famous Osceola." Isn't that something?

On Kenneth's father's side were a combination of Powhatan natives from Virginia, English settlers, and Montaukett from Montauk Long Island, New York. The Powhatan nation was a big confederacy, and Kenneth's ancestor from that tribe was his great-great-great-great-grandfather Black Feather. Black Feather was a chieftain of the Powhatan nation and made sure that the great sachem's orders were carried out. It was Black Feather who had married an English woman and acquired for the family the name Thompson.

Once, Kenneth's father wrote him a letter entitled "The Thompson Family: Its Beginning." The letter said that the family's history began in the late seventeen hundreds, with the marriage of Chief Black Feather, a Powhatan Chieftain of Jamestown, Virginia, to a white English settler, whose last name was Thompson. This marriage brought forth a son, Jacob. Jacob Thompson grew up in Virginia, Northampton County. As a young man, he left Virginia for New York. Jacob, being a seaman and later a captain, purchased land on Eastern Parkway, Rochester Avenue, in Brooklyn. There, he built a home.

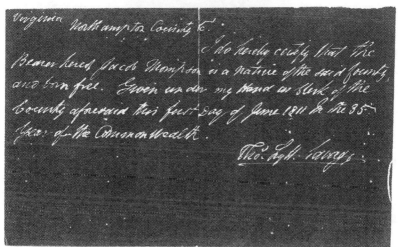

Captain Thompson sailed out of Brooklyn on his ship called, *The Jacobson*. Captain Thompson married a white English woman named Mary Baker. Jacob and Mary had four children—Jacob, Aaron, David, and Jeremiah.

Kenneth's great-grandfather, Jeremiah, was the only son who did not go to sea. He stayed at home with his mother. During his stay at home, he became engaged to Elizabeth Ellis, daughter of Dr. Elliis but his bride-to-be passed away. Grandfather Jeremiah attended Oberlin College to study medicine but did not finish. He had to return home to take care of his sick mother.

Whenever Captain Jacob Thompson returned home after being at sea for some time, he would bring home hogshead, flour, sugar, and molasses. He would give these items to the squatters on the land, who included the decedents of General Howe.

Jeremiah's brothers left Brooklyn and went their separate ways. One went to Oakland, California. Another migrated to Canada and married a French Canadian. One brother went to England and became a squire of England from their mother's inheritance. Upon the death of Harold's grandfathers' parents, their property was sold to the City of New York. Today, the ancestral home and property on Eastern Parkway is known as Lincoln Terrace Park.

*   *   *

Thinking of this and that, Kenneth remembered being addicted and homeless; it was Thanksgiving, and everyone was going to have a Thanksgiving feast. He'd had one too. He'd gone to the Salvation Army and sat and ate—broke bread with the other people who didn't have any means of putting together their own Thanksgiving meal. Talk about being humble and grateful, Kenneth was so grateful for this meal. Those were the type of things that made him a stronger and better person.

While Kenneth was homeless, he also had to try to support his drug habit. He would go to Labor Pool at four o'clock in the morning. Labor Pool was an agency that many homeless—alcoholics, drug addicts, and people in a bad position in life's storms—would go to in hopes of finding work each day. The jobs were first come, first serve and would start at 8:00 or 9:00 a.m. Whenever he went to work on a job site staffed by a group of men from Labor Pool, the workers were either intoxicated or high on drugs or not physically fit to do the kind of labor the job required. That was something.

After work, Kenneth would stop at a phone booth nearby the site before he made his way uptown to see his girlfriend, Carmen, where she lived with her mother, sisters, and brother.

One day, he called his father, who was on better terms with Kenneth by then, before heading to Carmen's. "Hi, Daddy."

"Hey, how are you doing, kid?" his father said.

"I'm doing well, Daddy. I just wanted to let you know everything's okay and I'm trying my best, and I just wanted to tell you I love you. I hope one day that you'll be proud of me."

"I hope so too, son," Harold replied. "Just be careful."

"Okay, Daddy. I'll talk to you soon, okay?"

"Okay, son."

Kenneth loved his father so much, and one of his major goals throughout the different storms he'd endured in life was for his father to, one day, be proud of him. And he knew that he was going to make that happen.

Taking the number one train, he arrived at 125th and Broadway, the stop before Kenneth's old shoeshine hustle. He decided to walk to Carmen's mother's apartment, where Carmen was staying. She lived between Broadway and Amsterdam Avenue on 122nd Street. It was a beautiful area, a nice neighborhood. The people who lived there came from all walks of life, which is what Kenneth liked. He liked everybody.

As he approached the building, he saw Carmen sitting on the steps. She was really beautiful, and she was just relaxing in casual clothing. You would never know that she was a dancer, and there wasn't anything wrong with that. He would find out later that she had also been a Playboy Bunny and a model. And while she had found employment in things that had to do with beauty, she had a nice personality. She just had other issues that bothered her.

Carmen took Kenneth's hand and they walked up to the top floor of the building to her Mom's apartment. Besides Carmen, her mom, sister, and brother, sometimes another sister stayed there too, but only off and on. Her mother was a casting agent, and she got people parts in movies or commercials or lined them up with modeling shoots—anything that had to do with entertainment. She got Kenneth his first part in a movie. He was an extra in *The Warriors*, a movie about a street gang that was on the run because of a misunderstanding; all the gangs in the city were after this one particular gang. United, the gangs had originally planned to take over the city, but instead, they decided to pursue the Warriors after a member of another gang blamed them for the death of the leader of all the gangs.

Kenneth was getting a welfare check at the time, as he had recently lost his job at Orange Julius. He used to accompany Carmen to her destination, wherever she was dancing, and then pick her up. When she was finished, he would be there. You could say he was her personal bodyguard. Coincidentally, when Harold had first known LaFawn, back in the Billie Holiday days, she was a dancer in the clubs, and Harold had been there for her before and after her work. Kenneth lived in a hotel room in midtown Manhattan, and he would go to the methadone program in the Bronx and then go hang out with Carmen back in Manhattan.

That's how things were for a while. Then Carmen's mother decided she was going to move further uptown. Because the apartment they were living in had been rented by the family for so many years, she decided to pass it on to Carmen. Wow, that was going to be nice. Carmen wanted Kenneth to live with her, and all he had to do was watch her back and to be in love with her. That was all.

Luckily for him, he wasn't a dummy, so he decided to go into sales. He got a nice job selling electronic scale systems for mail room and shipping departments. He worked for a company called Friden Mailing Equipment and competed against a company called Pitney Bowes, and he worked for a draw against commission. His territory was from 14th Street to Canal Street. It was a nice territory. The pace was an obstacle for Kenneth. Sales was a hustle—it was a fast-moving lifestyle. He dressed in nice suits; made a lot of money; and unfortunately, liked cocaine. He didn't like heroin anymore because he had to be up and moving quick. He liked the feeling that coke gave him. He would struggle with that obstacle for awhile.

Meanwhile, his girlfriend liked being on downers. After she finished dancing all night and while she was dancing, she liked to drink and take a lot of pills. So things were dysfunctional; even though he and Carmen thought they were having a fantastic time in life and were on top of the world, they weren't. There were many happy days and many sad days for Kenneth and Carmen. He often got jealous when he knew people were looking at his girlfriend as she danced erotically. He just couldn't help his feelings. But Carmen was doing what she wanted to do. And she was going to do it her way. Plus, she liked making a lot of money. She also liked spending a lot of money. She rarely took the subway, taking the train only when absolutely necessary. Everywhere she went, she took a cab. She and Kenneth also occasionally got into a fight because of Carmen being the center of attention wherever she went.

Kenneth just had that jealousy in his heart. He didn't like anybody staring at Carmen, and she used to get upset at that, really angry. She would always say, "Don't you know that I love you?"

"Yes," he would reply, "I know."

A lot of times though, she took advantage of him and others because of her beauty.

Carmen also had a wonderful heart, and she liked to laugh. She had two daughters, two wonderful little girls, and they were the joy in her life.The girls lived with Carmens aunt and grandmother She always wanted to be able to live with them and for them to be happy. Unfortunately, though, there was a problem in the family. It seems that her stepfather had raped her.

Carmen's real father didn't tolerate any type of negativity against his daughter or any of his loved ones. He was a gangster—and not just a wannabe. He was a high-level gangster, and he didn't play around. He was no joke. Carmen's father knew his daughter's lifestyle and the kind of work she did, as well as her drug problem. He liked cocaine and would always have some available. He knew all the people in the street world, his looks were versatile, and you never knew when he would appear. He also spoke Spanish because his family was from the Dominican Republic.

Carmen's father's name was Tito, and when he saw Kenneth, he didn't speak much. He said simply, "You just make sure you do the right thing for my daughter. You know what's going on. You know what time it is. You understand me?"

And Kenneth would reply, "Yes, I understand."

Tito would say, "Good. That's all I want you to do. Other than that, you're cool. You have no problem with me."

Well, Kenneth was surely glad to know that. He didn't want any problem with Tito. That was for sure.

Carmen was getting a lot of nice dancing gigs, and the tips were always good. Being so beautiful, she used to make a bundle. An agency booked her shows, ensuring that she had a regular week's schedule of work, and she performed at the top clubs all over the city. So it was nothing for her to make a few hundred a day, and she did have that spending habit, not to mention the pills. Kenneth was skimming from Carmen a bit off the top for the coke that he liked. He did tax expenses, if you catch the drift.

Carmen liked cocaine too, and they spent beyond their means, and were left without money for rent. This was before they lived permanently on 122nd Street. They were living in this place and that place, and the rent was always high. The drugs could make you spend your last and not even think about the rent, and before you knew it, you were out on the street with your bags or without your bags if the hotel held your belongings until you paid the rent for the room.

Luckily, they would get the money together and pay for some more days or a week at a time—most of the time. Sometimes it took a little while to get up the finances. The money situation was becoming a big problem. Carmen didn't like it, and Kenneth didn't like it. They had to do something, because the status quo just wasn't going to work.

PART THREE

THE SPLIT

Sales weren't like they used to be. The district manager decided that he wanted to hire college graduates who really didn't know anything about sales but had a college diploma. Kenneth, on the other hand, had been taught by the old-timers, when you really wore holes in your shoes and knocked on doors and never missed anything. He was able to communicate with presidents, vice Presidents of operations, and treasurers—every type of corporate member on any level—and show them the features, advantages, and benefits of the mailing equipment he sold. He had, after all, been taught by the best. One of those teachers was a very nice man, who was Kenneth's manager, Howie Lerner.

Kenneth would never forget Howie. Howie treated him well and taught him everything; he had a good heart. The two worked very well together; they shared a spiritual bond that couldn't be explained.

Howie retired, and soon thereafter, another, sales manager Ted McGuire, also left the company. The sales quota went up sky-high.

Each salesman had to sell more than $10, 500 worth of equipment every month. When Kenneth first heard this, his stomach tightened in pain. He briefly thought he had ulcers. Whenever he would worry about reaching his monthly quota, he would crouch low to the ground, the most comfortable spot for him until he felt better. A lot of months he did well, and sometimes he didn't. There were charge-backs and all kinds of corporate swindling going on. It was unbelievable. People would cut your throat for a sale.

Business wasn't always good with the dancing for Carmen, so she started to work at different places, such as old, established massage parlors, which was really in-house prostitution. The house would get a cut, and the girls would get a cut of all their business.

That's when Kenneth ran into associates he would later regret running into. He started hanging out with them and stealing, and on the side, they would hide girls who were trying to hide from their pimps. The girls would pay the guys to take them to another location to live and to make sure they were always safe from the pimp. The fellas also offered their services protecting parlors whenever one of the joints needed them for muscle. A lot of times, they were hired after the problem. They were getting paid all the time, from all ends. You can believe that there was money to be made, and these guys made it.

Carmen was messing around with this old man named Frank who owned a few adult movie houses. He had places in the city and even in upstate New York. Frank would buy Carmen anything she possibly wanted. All he wanted was her. He was ugly as hell, and he just wanted her as his "sex slave." He bought her everything that she wanted, even her pills, but he never gave her money, except a small allowance. He would keep her confined to close quarters, and she danced in his places—the adult movie houses. So he got his money back, believe me.

Kenneth and Carmen broke up. That was the split of the year; no one ever thought the two would break up. Kenneth started indulging in the cocaine way too much, and he returned to his old stomping grounds, the lower east side, to visit the different shooting galleries there. Whatever he made, he shot coke. It was 24-7; instead of the dope, it was the coke, constantly. He was trying to hold on to his job, which he knew he was going to lose soon.

One day, he just happened to walk into a prospect's place of business, the 13th Street Repertory company. The theater offered an apprentice type of membership; it was a repertory company that put on a variety of plays on stage and noted as the oldest off-Broadway company. As a 13th Street apprentice, you learned everything to do with theater, and that was something that Kenneth had always wanted to do. All the members had to put in a certain amount of hours every week and learn all areas of theater. Kenneth spoke about the apprenticeship with the director. The theater wasn't interested in mailing equipment, but there was a possibility of an open door for Kenneth with his acting career. He thanked the director of the theater for talking to him and said that he would be in touch, and they parted, telling one another to have a good day.

Kenneth was reminiscing one evening as he was walking down the street; he started to think about how ruthless his ex- I repeat, ex-associates and partners in crime were. They were cold, greedy and unpredictable. They had heart when it came to committing crimes, but they lacked heart when it came to compassion. One of the reasons he had split from them was that, at one time, he'd had to prevent his associates from a seriously horrific endeavor. They were pretending they liked this young lady and her friends, making plans to hang out with the girls. But their real plan was to take the girls to her home and rape her and her friends and rob them. Kenneth wasn't going to tolerate that at all. He had told his partners when they were sitting in the two cabs—quietly because the women were right next to them in the other cab—"If you do anything at all to them, I have my piece also, and we'll just have a shootout right here. I'm not kidding! You better leave her and her friends alone."

His "friends" had obliged, knowing that he was serious. They'd paid the cab driver that the ladies were in and said goodnight. That was a close call. Somebody was going to get shot, and Kenneth didn't plan on it being him. He had it in his heart, though, to help people who weren't able to help themselves in certain situations. He had that compassion in his heart.

Oh, God, please help me out of these problems in life. Please let me get out of this darkness. Please let me see the light. Oh, Lord, help me. Those were the type of thoughts that Kenneth quite frequently had. And he would speak to the Lord; he had that type of relationship with God.

* * *

About a year had passed since Carmen and Kenneth had split up. He had continued going to different places where he knew she would be appearing when she wasn't upstate, and they slowly got back together. By then she had the apartment that her mother had said she was going to pass on to her when she moved. Kenneth moved in with Carmen, and things got a little bit better as far as their relationship and their love for each other. He felt good again, and he hoped that she did too.

Things were looking up in sales too. Due to corporate, political changes, Kenneth no longer worked for the company selling electronic scale systems. He now worked for Minolta business systems selling photocopiers. That job went really well until he started noticing an unsettling pattern. His manager always seemed to want to go with him on the big jobs that Kenneth was getting ready to close—the prospects with who he would make a nice commission and wouldn't have to worry about any quotas. After the meetings, a few days later his manager would, all of a sudden, tell him that his prospect had decided to go with the competitor, like Xerox or IBM. This started happening very often.

One day, not to be a mean guy but to get straight to the point, Kenneth told his manager, "Let me tell you something; if I find out that you're stealing any of my business, you're going to end up right in the river, and I'm not kidding. You'll end up right in that East River. I work hard, and I try to make a living. And If I find out that you're stealing, you're done."

That job went soon after that because the manager wasn't going to feel uncomfortable and threatened, and he knew he was stealing. So Kenneth decided to do whatever he could. Sometimes he sold pills or sometimes he'd get some wholesale products and sell them a little under retail.

His girlfriend, too, took a variety of jobs. She worked in parlors and danced and, occasionally, she had some special customers who would take very good care of her. I guess you would call them Sugar Daddies. But even when she was doing well, she wasn't going to give up all her money. She had a big, expensive appetite for the luxuries in life. She would let Kenneth hold on to some money, and he would definitely tax her on that drug he liked, cocaine. Again and again, that's where the money secretly dwindled away—on that drug and on her drug. They would also get high together, sniffing coke. So they never really got that far, even though they made the big bucks.

Kenneth would sometimes bring his girlfriend to visit his father and stepmother in Quogue, Long Island, on Riverside Drive, where his parents had moved from the city. They'd sold their condo and built a beautiful, two-story house off Quantauk Creek. An animal reserve was nearby, so you always saw all types of birds. As a matter of fact, one of the things that Kenneth liked to do when he visited his parents was buy a hundred pounds of cracked corn and spread it from the beginning of their dock and all over the yard. The yard would fill with different birds; what a sight to see. Kenneth's stepmom loved to see the birds in the yard too. She would watch from her kitchen, which was on the top floor. His relationship with his parents was better again.

Carmen didn't really click with them, though, because she always seemed like she was bored. Plus, she was interested in those pills, and sometimes when they visited, she would be out of some and not feel very comfortable. So you couldn't really blame her for feeling miserable if she was sick and needed some drugs.

*   *   *

It was Memorial Day weekend, and Kenneth was walking down the street looking at everyone hustling and bustling everywhere—all returning from wherever they had spent their weekend, with their loved ones or elsewhere. He was reminiscing about times when Carmen's dancing business was kind of shaky; he had to think of something else to do, mainly for her benefit and so he could skim off the top.

He noticed a newsstand with adult newspapers on the side of the stand. He bought one and looked through it. Besides the stories and graphics, the paper also had advertisements. The ads were for different types of agencies (outcall services). This was a lot different from the setup for the street women of the evening—this was a different level. The women who worked with most of the agencies were top class, at least the women Kenneth was interested in.

So he discussed opening up an agency with Carmen, and she thought it was a great idea. First, they had to come up with a name. Kenneth looked at Carmen for a moment, and then it clicked. "Eye Catchers," he suggested.

Eye Catchers had a nice sound, and it certainly related to beauty and to the subject at hand.

Next, they drew up some artwork with the help of a printer. They came up with a beautiful eye next to the words "Eye Catchers." The logo had a very classy look. So Kenneth paid for the newspaper ad, making sure he had the size and location within the newspaper that he wanted. Now he had a connection with the outside world. In addition, he printed business cards and spread them around to all the high-class joints.

Carmen bought a few new outfits and new allure 100 percent human hair wig's and shoes, of course. She was going to be on call, taking whatever calls she either fit the description for or wanted to go on. That was her choice and free will.

Next, Kenneth interviewed people who had answered various parts of the ad. Carmen also conducted interviews; she talked with the ladies, and Kenneth left that part mainly up to her.

Carmen decided her name in the business would be Cat Woman. Kenneth decided to use the name Nick, NY Nick, or Nick Neapalotano. The aliases were part of the business; this was another adventure, and everything was on the down low. Nobody ever got hurt, which was a good thing.

Next, Nick hired drivers—a father and son team. These were professional drivers in all areas. They had licenses to carry firearms as professional bodyguards. And they had with them at all times trained Doberman pinschers. The dogs would go with them and the female escort to the location, and the driver and the dog would wait. The client would pay by the hour; and the driver, the young lady, and the agency would split up everything by percentages and occasional bonuses from the agency.

It was really a smooth operation. Things were really rolling. Soon, it was nothing to make a few grand a day. There were slow days too, but on those days, hey, they had fun, and Cat Woman did spend some money.

Charlie and Pete were great drivers. They were reliable, punctual, on point, and very protective of everyone with Eye Catchers. They made sure that things were always safe plus. In addition, Nick and Cat Woman had everyone on voice beepers and made sure that, as soon as the lady or ladies got to their location, they would call the office. The drivers would also check in with Nick or Cat Woman when they were leaving. Sometimes, Cat Woman went on calls—those were top dollar and with clients who requested only her.

The best thing about the out-call business was that, as long as you had the right ladies, you would always have a steady clientele. Everyone was thoroughly interviewed, and it wasn't just their looks that got them hired. They were also chosen for their intelligence level, honor, and respect. Nick wouldn't have it any other way. In addition, if any problem ever arose, there was always backup along with the father and son driver team. If Nick had to appear due to a problem, he would.

Very rarely were there any problems, though. Eye Catchers clients were harmless, if crazy. One customer liked to watch two or more ladies wrestle while he freebased, a term for smoking cocaine. This particular client liked petite, athletic young ladies. They would put on a show for the guy, wrestling for anywhere from two to ten hours. In addition, the guy would do some business with one of the drivers for more coke. As long as he had coke, the more hours the ladies would stay. Getting paid by the hour earned everyone quite a nice dollar, and the best thing about it was that the pay was always in cash. The ladies always got very good tips also. Nothing, however, was done without the agency. No feelings were involved and no strings attached. That's what the clients wanted—strictly professional. Nick and Cat Woman only experienced good business and a lot of money. They had a few favorite ladies who would get the clients to go further than the one hour they were hired for. That's where sales abilities and intelligence came into play.

One of the favorites was Brandy. Most of the time, her hour appointment would turn into a few more hours and, sometimes, an overnight, twenty-four-hour call. Having a worker like that was very lucrative. Nick paid special attention to these workers, increasing their cut with a higher percentage. Cat Woman would focus on the ladies who didn't get call backs often. These women would either stick it out and things would get better or they would leave the agency and, usually, go back to the street to work. There were never any hard feelings if things didn't work out between a lady and the agency. They made their own decisions, and the agency wasn't their pimp. So nobody was forced to do or not do anything. First-impression-last-impression effect was important.

Nick would go to most of ladies' homes so he could see their surroundings and determine whether there were any obstacles that seemed negative. He noticed an interesting thing about Brandy, which was really none of his business. Their best worker, believe it or not, would take her cash home to her grandfather. She had told Cat Woman about this when they went on a call together. Nick didn't know what the story was, and he didn't ask any questions. What he did know was that Brandy was good with them.

Nick made a point to meet the new employees. Often, he would pop up when they were finished with a client or Nick would ask the driver to meet him with the lady after the call. He'd see how the drivers were doing and that everything was everything. He'd get paid right there, and the drivers would give him the take for the whole day so far. Hopefully, there would be more, later. He did this also because he had some questions concerning his drivers; he wanted to make sure he grabbed the money as quickly as he could, especially when it was busy.

No one knew Nick and Cat Woman's location, for more than one reason. Eye Catcher's wasn't a nine-to-five type of business; it was a twenty-four hour on call operation that depended on phone calls, advertising, repeats, and word of mouth. What part of the year it was also affected business. Holidays were always good. And the economy was a factor.

Thing's weren't always as good as they'd expected, though. As a matter of fact, business eventually got really bad. After awhile, it got so slow that the ladies were going on call with a few agencies at the same time. Cat Woman started to take all the jobs. Who could blame her? It was all about survival. Soon, very few ladies were on call with the service. Cat Woman would get what she could from the agency and then go to an in-house parlorr. Nick never forced her to do anything. Whatever Carmen did, she wanted to do it. He never got physical with her unless she had done so first, a result of being drunk, high, and stressed out—when the other side of her split personality would come out.

Regardless of how Carmen was behaving, Kenneth watched her back, just as he did with anyone he felt close to in his life. Kenneth always made sure that, for people who were in his corner, he would be in theirs.

The thing that disturbed him most was that Carmen would change too much. When she would take on one of her personalities, she would go out and not return for a few days, sometimes even a week or two. When she'd come back, she'd tell some outrageous story to explain her absence. Once, she claimed that she'd been kidnapped and had had no way of getting back. She said she'd called home but no one had answered and that she had been able to escape from the kidnappers. She really thought she played the whole thing off with a top performance. But Kenneth didn't think she was telling the truth. He had a feeling that she was seeing somebody, and Kenneth would find out later that she was, indeed, starting to.

One of Carmen's fans became one of her lovers. That's how life was sometimes.

*　　*　　*

Just before the agency opened, Carmen was dancing at a club, and Kenneth had a horrifying two days he would never forget. Carmen went to Baltimore with her cousin, who was also a stripper and dancer. They were going to be away for a week to dance at a top club there. Kenneth stayed back in New York. Due to his addictive behavior, he got the urge to check into a hotel—not an expensive one but one in midtown Manhattan. Then he went to 9th Avenue to buy some cocaine. He went back to the room after he'd copped (slang for bought) and had gone to the store to pick up some fluids to drink, cigarettes, and snacks. Back in the hotel room, he planned to call it a night, relax and get high. He really wasn't able to relax though as he proceeded to shoot up. He had five bags to start with, one at a time if it was good.

The coke was real good, top shelf. The only thing that Kenneth experienced was that his money was going quick because, after the five dimes,(ten dollar bags) he went back to 9th Avenue and bought some more coke. This time, he bought seven bags; now that was a lot of coke. He planned to be shooting up for a while. Not being greedy, he liked to shoot one dime at a time.

He started to get paranoid. He thought that the police were going to bust down the door and arrest him. He kept looking under the door, putting his ear to it. He tried to sleep, but that didn't work. He watched television as long as he could and then shot another dime after he had calmed down a little bit. The beers he had brought with him helped him calm down a little.

Soon, though, the paranoia was getting worse. It was unbelievable; he felt he was going through a living horror—something he wouldn't want anyone to experience. Then in addition to thinking that the police were going to come, he also thought that somebody else might be after him. He was really skitzing. And, ironically, after he would calm himself down, he would shoot another dime, starting the cycle all over again.

He went broke quickly—in just two days. He couldn't sleep at all and went through a horrible few days. He didn't really spend every dime he had at the end of that run because Carmen used to make sure that he had a few bucks for this and that. But the food money was of no interest to Kenneth. He wanted to shoot it; that was his meal. He ended up really going hungry; the only thing he ate was some pork crackling with rice and garlic. He didn't learn then, but he did ask God to please guide him out of the living hell on earth.

He liked the cocaine, and he didn't like the cocaine. This was a constant feeling in his head, and he was becoming uncomfortable. He was just getting by, by the skin of his teeth, with not getting arrested. The police weren't watching him specifically, but the areas he would go to were hot.

In a way what helped him was opening up Eye Catchers. The agency was strictly business, and he went back to just sniffing. And when the business and the cash flow was good, this worked.

Even through that, Carmen's personality changes were difficult, especially when she would hang out with a neighbor and drink with her. Mix that with pills and then try to do business. Things would really get ugly—with customers, with the other ladies, and with the drivers; everything would be off balance. Such situations were one of Kenneth's triggers; when the balance tipped, he would turn to coke. It was an escape. And then, when he was broke, he would always regret what he'd done and felt guilty.

Kenneth would never forget an incident that occurred before he and Carmen had started the service. The couple was walking on 8th Avenue in midtown Manhattan. Kenneth went into a store for a few minutes while Carmen waited outside. When he came out, she appeared from around the comer. "Hey, listen," she told him, "I just got two customers together. They're right around the corner in the parking lot."

"Okay, let's check them out, and we'll take it from there," Kenneth said.

They went to the parking lot and approached the car where the two brothers were waiting. They got into the car to talk business, explaining that, of course, getting the money up front, especially with two Johns, would be great. All of a sudden, the situation turned from falsely good to real evil. The two guys started punching both Kenneth and Carmen as soon as the men had paid Carmen and locked the doors. Kenneth and Carmen punched back, and there was a big scuffle. Eventually, they were able to unlock the front door and get out the car. They had gotten the money up front, so that was another thing they had on the thugs. They were lucky to get back into the light, where there was traffic and people, which made them feel safer. They kept running and running and didn't feel at ease until they'd made it back to the hotel where they were staying. That was one of the incidents that had motivated Kenneth to do something on a different level-one of the precursors to Eye Catchers.

But even during that venture, Nick started to get a funny feeling. He was concerned about the drivers. Some of the answers the son gave when it was time to meet up with him were kind of fishy. The father would rarely say anything more than, "Whatever you say, Nick." He started to suspect that they were police officers and that he was getting set up. Perhaps these guys were bideing their time, trying to get that big bust. Or maybe he was just paranoid. Whatever the case, Nick was extra careful, and he watched everyone closely.

He also had to keep a close eye on Carmen. When she was out of hand, he didn't let her do anything that had to do with business. He would rather see her not on anything or passed out than to ruin business. As business slowed, money got tight.

One regular difficulty Nick had to face with Cat Woman was her defiance. She kept returning to one client's home, despite the fact that Nick had asked her repeatedly not to go. The John lived on the east side of midtown Manhattan, in an area that housed a group of nice condo apartments. One time, Nick got a call from her. Screaming, she told him to get over to the location and to bring an ax.

Nick didn't even bother going there; he told her to just jump in a cab and that they'd talk about it when she got home. When she arrived, she was furious. Nick could tell she was wasted on alcohol, pills, and cocaine. She said that the guy owed her money and he wasn't going to give it to her. She demanded that Nick go there with an ax, chop the door down, and get the money from him. He didn't want anything to do with any type of negative actions. For one thing he was on the DL, and he certainly didn't need a spotlight of attention on him. Pursuing finances that way wasn't going to help anything.

But he loved her and realized she wasn't going to stop, and he was afraid she was going to do something even crazier. So, believe it or not, he went to the hardware store and bought an ax. Cat Woman showed him where the place was, and he swung the ax against the door. He didn't hack it down though; it was metal, so all he did was dent it. Not getting anywhere, he started swinging at the doorknob. But that didn't work either, and it was getting loud. He knew that, if he didn't leave right away, he was going to get arrested or the person on the other side of that door might come out and kill him.

From what Cat Woman had told him, the guy owed her half money and half cocaine. Between the product and the money, that came out to quite a bit, as she had been there for twenty hours. This guy wasn't the ordinary Joe.

That was one of the last experiences Kenneth and Carmen shared before they parted. Kenneth knew then that things between them weren't going to work too much longer. He also had his own problems with his addiction. When there were problems like that, he wanted some coke—not just to sniff but to shoot—and he spent a lot of money. When money was short, they would start arguing. Their love got hectic and out of control. Only the love—that crazy love—kept them together, until they finally parted ways.

* * *

Who knew that being in love could make a man attempt to take his own life? That's what Kenneth did. Carmen was going to leave him, and to show her how much he loved her, he attempted to cut both of his jugular veins. He ended up going to the hospital in an ambulance.

The emergency room staff was prepared to admit him and put him under mental observation. He told them that he was all right, explaining why he had done it and assuring them that he wouldn't do it again. Looking back, Kenneth would later understand what a crazy thing it was for anyone to try and kill themselves. Plus, taking one's own life was a sin; that was what Kenneth was raised to believe.

The incident stemmed from a lack of finances. Once again, Kenneth and Carmen didn't have any money and the rent was due. Carmen went on a rampage, threatening to leave him. She had done this before and had always gone back to him, but this time felt different; it felt real. The first thing that Kenneth thought of was cutting his neck. Isn't that crazy? He cut his neck on both sides near where the jugular veins lay. He could have bled to death, but he wasn't thinking about that because he was in love. The crazy part was that now he had to walk around all bandaged up and looking like a fool. Carmen didn't respect that she was playing with his feelings and making him weak mentally. When it came to his love for her, he was often weak. He had to put that weakness aside if he was going to survive, especially around her.

Things are different right now. We're in a little slump, but we're going to make it to the top. That's what Kenneth thought. In his ignorance, he believed they were going to become millionaires. Anything may be possible, but it wasn't going to be for them. His dreams of their business succeeding and their financial worries ending would never be reality.

Cause and effect played its role for Kenneth and Carmen. They couldn't even afford to pay for the advertisement for their business, much less the rent. They were concentrating on the drugs and alcohol that they wanted. Business got slower and slower. He had to politely tell the drivers that he wouldn't need their services any longer, as he was getting out of the picture. They shook hands, and that was the end of his dealings with the father and son. He also told the ladies that, as they all knew, business was just about to a halt and that they should pursue their endeavors with another agency or finding something progressive in their life that would be better for their well-being.

Spiritual cause and effect was working, and now the darkness came out as dark as the night. Kenneth's relationship with Carmen was getting worse and worse. Neighbors, alcohol, sex, and drugs got involved and caused a negative effect. Stealing from each other didn't help.

Carmen also had a secret admirer. One day, after they had split up for only a day or two, Kenneth came home and this guy answered the door. Kenneth knew the guy from the street world, and Kenneth simply asked him what he was doing there and told him to leave. The guy left without any problems.

Kenneth stayed with Carmen that night, and they made love and discussed how things had gotten where they were. They talked about their relationship and the business. And they decided to part ways and still respect each other.

PART FOUR

ENLIGHTENMENT

Once Nick and Cat Woman finally, for the last time, split up and went their separate ways, the transition for Nick started.

Kenneth decided to go to upstate New York for awhile and work. He got the job through an agency and went to a resort that had been converted to a senior citizen residence, working as a pot washer, busboy, and assistant food server and taking care of other odds and ends at the establishment. He loved being around the people. To him, interacting with them was a form of spirituality and enlightenment. He always gave the senior residents the utmost, highest respect.

The residents would talk to Kenneth, and they would sometimes vent a few complaints. Many of them felt they were being poisoned because too many people there were dying. Kenneth did notice, without reaching a conclusion, that there was quite a bit of ambulance activity at the residence. As far as he knew, the people were elderly and died of individual medical or natural circumstances.

Two things did give Kenneth pause though. When he helped the chef with the stockpot that they made soup in, he noticed that some of the meat looked spoiled. In addition, he saw that the chef put the chicken in the pot with the metal labels still on the meat. Another thing that made Kenneth question what was going on at the facility came to his attention when he was completing an odd job he'd been assigned. He was to clean out a storage refrigerator. For one thing, a lot of the meat in the fridge was rotten, and the walls were green and dirty. He cleaned out everything very thoroughly and threw most of the meat away, so that it wouldn't end up being used and causing anyone to get sick or die. He threatened the residence owners that he would report them to the media for these things, and he was soon terminated from that job.

Losing that job was just as well because, besides the problems with the facility, Kenneth had a roommate who was an alcoholic and made threats sometimes when the booze was talking through him.

He decided to go back to the city and visit the director of 13th Street Repertory.

*   *   *

THE 13th ST. THEATER
50 West 13th Street
675-6677

Kenneth was single now; he had to keep reminding himself of that. So he would have time to pursue his dream in show business. Learning that he had a special gift that would still be discovered by himself and others was a wonderful thing.

Once Kenneth spoke to the director again and discussed the apprenticeship membership with the repertory company, he was accepted. He asked her if he could rent a room or even a spot anywhere, as he didn't have any place to live. He suggested that, with such a situation, he could learn as much as possible and pay her whatever the rent was whenever he could. He did have some money to give her in advance for a few weeks. She said he could stay there and told him that she saw something special in him—a connection between him and the arts.

Kenneth would never forget the people who helped him when he first started on stage and as a member of the repertory company. Kenneth was one of the few minorities in the company. Being at the theatre with everyone together gave Kenneth a great feeling—it felt like family.

He enjoyed learning all areas of the theatre and always put in more than the three hours required of all the members. This work was enjoyable and a natural high. The first thing Kenneth learned was to work as a lighting and sound technician. He also did voice-over in a play as a train conductor, announcing the train stops. In addition, he got a small part in the same play, *The Seekers*, as a cab driver.

Performing the combined roles was interesting. He would change the lighting cue to a set position for the scene he was in, go over the theatre's roof and down a flight of stairs, and be on the stage on time for his appearance as a cab driver. His role started by carrying the baggage of a woman and her friend up two flights of stairs. The friend, who was visiting, would say, "Thank you," and hand him a dime.

The cabbie would look at the dime in his hand and say, "What's this, lady?"

She would say, "You've been very nice and that's your tip."

"Nice is nice, but I got to make a living," he'd reply. "You can't eat with nice, and you can't pay your bills with nice, and I'm not leaving until I get a decent tip."

The visitor's girlfriend would hand him a dollar, and he'd reply, "Gee thanks, lady. Hey, lady, do me a favor; teach your girlfriend some manners." And he'd exit slamming the door behind him.

At that exit, Kenneth would go over the roof for the next lighting cue. That was a lot of fun.

At night, he'd sleep in one of the rooms where they had met earlier for a class with one of the directors or to going over lines in a rehearsal or for a reading discussion.

One night, he enjoyed playing Christopher Cross's song, "Fly Like the Wind," and went to sleep on the stage just to feel the feeling he got there and take in atmosphere and spirit of the theatre—the hundreds, perhaps thousands of feet, that had performed on that stage. What a wonderful, enlightening experience.

During the early part of the days, when Kenneth had a few hours of free time, he'd earn some money by going to wholesale stores and buying an item by the dozen that was selling fast in the retail stores. He would sell the product a little under its retail price. That was a very quick way to make money. He'd be a walking salesman until he sold out, and if he had more time that day, he'd do it again and make his profit. He liked a hustle like that so he could finish quickly and return quickly to the place he loved—the theatre. He was finally free to do something he wanted to do.

Things must have happened the way they did because that's how they were supposed to happen. Kenneth always felt that things happened the way the Lord intended them to. That was a good thing to feel. He believed so much that he knew it was real—that relationship that he had with God.

One time, during the Christmas season, Kenneth was selling hat and a scarf sets, one size fits all, for five dollars, and they went like hotcakes. He just happened to see Carmen and her boyfriend walking by. He called them over, his attitude pleasant. "Hi," he said. "I just want to give you two a Christmas gift." He gave them each a hat and scarf set.

They said thank you and wished each other well before saying good-bye. That was the way it was supposed to be, instead of things ending completely negative. It could have been the other way, and that would have been ugly. Who wants to end a relationship ugly? After all, Kenneth and Carmen had, at one time, been in love, and then they'd parted. So it was best to wish each other well, instead of badly.

*   *   *

In 1979, Ken had the opportunity to be in his first play that was an off-off-Broadway show at Studio R. Experimental TV Workshop. The play was called *Our Dear Wife*, and Kenneth played a character named Larry. The story was about four people. Two were dead—Larry, who Ken was playing, and Jeff. Both of them had been killed by their former wife, Janet. Janet had a new husband named Joe, who she was planning to kill as well. The motive for each murder, of course, was her husbands' money; both Larry and Jeff had had very big insurance policies.

In order for Larry and Jeff to get their wings and get out of purgatory, they had to convince Joe of Janet's plan. They also had to scare Janet and convince her to stop doing the wrong things in life—to repent to God.

The play was very interesting and complex. Being very close to the audience without eye contact was an interesting experience for Ken. For most of his part, he was sitting on a swing in purgatory with Jeff, and the two were looking down on earth as ghosts.

To make a long story short, Larry and Jeff they did end up getting their wings. Janet repented, but she still had to wait a long time before she was going to get any answer from God. And Joe was saved.

About a year, laterhe rediscovered himself at the 13th Street Repertory and did the show *The Seekers* for quite awhile. He stayed with the company until he'd seen, learned, and listened as much as he could in theatre.

*   *   *

For Ken, being at the theater was like being enrolled in a school for acting. He stuck with the director, and with whatever she did, he learned something from her. And she loved teaching him. He was like a special student to her at; least that's how Ken felt.

The first big show Ken felt ready to audition for was *The Indian Wants the Bronx* by Israel Horovitz. The play wasn't about an American Indian; it was about a Hindu Indian who was stranded in this country and, somehow, separated from his son, Prem.

Unable to find his son, the father tries to call all kinds of numbers that he doesn't know. Confused, he calls out his son's name, "Prem,

Prem," speaking in Hindi in a panic. Suddenly, these two street punks, Murph and Joey, from the neighborhood appear. Murph yells to Joey, "Hey look at the Indian." And the two start teasing the man and banging on the telephone booth. They harass him until he is filled with terror. In the end, they stab him. The dying Indian would never find his son because these two street punks shortened his life—in part because the man was foreign and in part because Murph and Joey were two punks who just liked negativity.

Ken auditioned for Murph's role for the versatility, but Murph was Irish and Ken was Native American, so that wasn't going to work. However, he was pleased to audition for and land the starring role as the Indian.

Ken liked his routine. He would get up, do chores around the theatre, go to rehearsals and acting classes, and put in a few hours if he could to make money to survive. He loved eating falafels because they were inexpensive and healthy. He liked pizza too because it was filling. You couldn't beat Ray's Pizza at that time; it was the best. People used to stand in a big line just to get a few slices of that pizza. Ken spent his days and nights at the theatre and went to sleep there. He always thanked God for everything—for allowing him to begin to fulfill his dreams to be in shows and for guiding him with spiritual balance.

In 1968, Israel Horovitz won an Obie for *The Indian Wants the Bronx*, starring Al Pacino. Horovitz is a prolific writer, and his plays have been performed all over the world in many languages.

His talents include screenwriting and teaching playwriting. His film, *Author, Author*, also starring Al Pacino, was released in 1982.

Seven of his plays, under the heading of *The Wakefield Plays*, were published by Avon Books and performed at the Public Theatre. The Public also did *Sunday Runners in the Rain*, also performed in Los Angeles. His off-Broadway play, *The Good Parts*, starring Tony Roberts, ran at the Astor Place Theatre in 1981.

Line was, at one time the longest-running off-off-Broadway play, showing for seven years at the 13th Street Theatre.

*   *   *

Don't get the wrong picture; even though Ken loved the theatre and everyone in the repertory company, there were some tough days. The tough days included rehearsals, learning lines as quickly as possible, and learning different choreography. At the introduction of a new play, the actors would be taught everything first in a classroom. Then the rehearsal would move from the room to the stage, where everyone would continue learning his or her lines and where to be on stage during different scenes. They would continue as if it were a show with the audience watching. The director would be the only audience in rehearsal until the show was perfected for a real performance.

One of the next shows that Ken really enjoyed was *The Empire Laughs Back*, a spin-off from The Emperor's New Clothes. *The Empire Laughs Back* had two characters, who were actors, Peachy and Bubbles. Ken played Peachy, and a young lady in the repertory company, Lisa, played Bubbles. Peachy and Bubbles had such a good time as actors in the emperor's royal court. One of their parts was to show the emperor how great he looked in his celestial robes, diamonds, emerald, and rubies. In actuality, the emperor didn't have any clothes on at all. He was in his underwear—that was the funny part.

EDITH O'HARA and THE THIRTEENTH STREET THEATRE are proud to present
a Jolly, Holly, Mistletoe-tapping Christmas special:

(a tiny musical)

Directed by ROBERTA HAWKINS

Based upon the book "A CHRISTMAS CAROL" by CHARLES DICKENS

Text by MICHAEL MACINA

Musical Adaptation by MICHAEL MACINA, JACK MESSINGER,

RONNIE WISEMAN, and PAUL ROBERTSON

with

BOB HECK, KEN THOMPSON, JOHN AGNELLO, PAT DENISTRAN,

CHARLES NICHOLSON, DAVID HOLBROOK, CLAIRE CLARK,

ANISH JAIN, and PAUL ROBERTSON

Costumes - SUSAN SAYERS   Sets - KIRK DUNCAN   Lights - LYNNE HIETT
Produced by THE THIRTEENTH STREET THEATRE, in co-operation with
VIDEO CABARET INTERNATIONAL, and MICHAEL HOLLINGSWORTH

-performances-

12/15, 4:30 p.m.; 12/16, 4:30 p.m.; 12/17, 11:00 p.m.; 12/22, 4:30 &
9:30; 12/24, 2:00; 12/26, 5:00; 12/29, 4:30 and 9:30; 12/30, 4:30;
12/31, 11:00; 1/1/83, 5:00; 1/2/83, 5:00 CALL 675-6677 / $6.00
Children $3

Doing that show was very enjoyable, and Ken loved it even more because it was a performance for children and they loved it. The children's shows were on Saturdays and Sundays, the first shows of the day. Often, there was also a special birthday party for one of the children, and the birthday boy or girl would be accompanied by friends and parents. After the show, the cast would come out still in costume and sing "Happy Birthday" and have cake and ice cream with everyone.

After *The Empire Laughs Back*, Ken decided to learn musicals, drama, and comedy. He wanted to know and be versatile in all areas of acting. One of the interesting parts he played next was Jacob Marley in the musical *Scrooge*. Jacob Marley was in chains, and he was already deceased. As everyone most likely knows, he haunted Scrooge. Ken enjoyed rising from a trapdoor in the floor when he heard his cue and scaring the heck out of Scrooge. In chains with his skin painted all white, he definitely did look deceased, and he would start to sing a song about himself being in chains, telling Scrooge different things about himself. *Scrooge* was quite a success, and Ken's director for the show gave him a letter to include with his acting résumé when he went on auditions or interviews.

The letter read:

January 6, 1983

Ken Thompson played Jacob Marley in the 1982 13th Street Repertory production of *Scrooge*, which I directed. I found him to be personable, cooperative and hardworking. His professional attitude was evident in his punctuality, reliability and willingness to accept direction. He got along well with others in the cast and his technical assistance was beyond the call of duty. His generosity with his time and support contributed much to the overall production. Ken is secure and relaxed on stage. His speaking voice is rich and flexible, and though his singing voice is untrained, it is controlled and powerful. His acting adjustments are smooth, quick and justified. He works well with given circumstances and plays a strong objective. He captured the character of Marley and gave a well rounded serious-comic performance, which carefully incorporated ghostly intimidation with comfortable familiarity. It was a clever choice and his portrayal was a high point in the show. I also saw him play Gupta in *The Indian Wants the Bronx*. I was amazed at his range of characterization. This vulnerable, naive old Indian was a full spectrum away from Jacob Marley—physically, vocally and emotionally. Because of his versatility, personality and dedication, Ken Thompson is an asset to any production and particularly valuable to a repertory company. I would gladly cast him again and would strongly recommend him to another director.

Sincerely,
Roberta Hawkins

Saturdays and Sundays were busy for Kenneth at the theater. He got another role for a children's show, which meant that, in the early part of the day, he would do one of the shows and then, in the early afternoon, the other children's show. In this production, *The Snow White Show*, Kenneth played a woodsman, a prince, a cowboy, a cool dwarf, and a magic mirror. He enjoyed every part he played, taking in the humor while, as the magic mirror, he told the queen how beautiful she looked, even though she was really very ugly.

The cool dwarf was a fun role too. Ken would pick children from the audience, especially the birthday boy or girl. They would be cool dwarfs, snapping their fingers and making fun and laughing along with Ken, the big dwarf, about the ugly queen and vowing to protect Snow White. He had quite a lot of fun with the audience participation.

One night while Kenneth was upstairs in the lighting and sound booth hanging out with the technician for the show being rehearsed, he got curious. He had never seen this musical and asked about its name. Ed, the tech, said the show was called *The Thing That Ate Syracuse*. What had really gotten Kenneth's attention were the costumes and masks—everyone had on full masks and wigs. One of the actors, Nancy, played a character named Professor Fred. In costume and mask, "the professor" looked like an old man with whiskers and glasses; "he" was always writing a formula on an invention he was working on. With the masks and elaborate characters and the superb acting, the show was magical.

The show had originally been called *The Mask Show* and was later changed to *The Thing That Ate Syracuse*, titled after a main character, a robot named Dagostino. You see, the professor's granddaughter, Jessica, had everything, and she still wan't satisfied. So he gets busy in his workshop and invents Dagostino, who would be able to do anything her heart desired and follow her every command. Unfortunately, Dagostino eventually goes a little crazy and ends up eating everything in Syracuse.

Nancy, the actor who played Professor Fred, was very attractive. She was another thing that had triggered Ken's attention to the show; that and her voice. He started to talk to Nancy and to show up at all the rehearsals for that show. Then he auditioned for the part of Professor Fred and got the role. Each show had more than one cast, so he wasn't interfering with anyone who was already doing the show. He was an understudy for Professor Fred's part until Nancy left the show later to pursue another major part.

Ken learned the lines and songs for *Syracuse* quickly. He looked forward to transforming into an old man in costume and mask for each performance; it was so real and a lot of fun.

At night—when everything was quiet and the last show was over, the theatre was swept and cleaned and the garbage emptied, and all the proceeds for the day had been counted and put away for the director to take when she came downstairs from her apartment—whoever was up last would also make sure the theater was locked for the night. The same thing went for the morning if the director wasn't up yet; Ken or one of the other actors who lived at the theater would open up. The key was kept in a specific location. Everyone did what they were doing because of the love of being there. Kenneth felt blessed that he was able to live, learn, participate, and perform at the theater.

Things did start changing for Ken once his mind-set changed. He always wanted to do the right thing. It just so happened that he had a lot of dark obstacles following him; and it seemed that people, places, and things would never line up quite right. It was as if someone had put a spell on him, blocking things from falling in line for him. However, Ken's faith in the Lord got that spell—if that's what was blocking his path—taken away. He wasn't going to let anything or anyone block his path or goals.

In his spare time, which wasn't very often, Ken would go and dance at different clubs all night to unwind. Sometime he would sit in Washington Square Park and listen to the music playing and hang out and communicate with everyone—keeping it real. His spirit was free, and he had the freedom to be able to do things that were positive and creative, climbing levels in life.

His parents were also proud of him. Theatre was one of the things Ken's father had thought he would be good at and should pursue instead of living and being in the street world of darkness. Well his father's wish came true, and now Harold was starting to be proud of his son like he'd always wanted to be. Kenneth was so happy that his father and stepmother were finally proud of him. He loved to go to Quogue, Long Island, where his parents lived and visit when he could. They would discuss what was going on at the theater, and Kenneth also liked walking to the animal wildlife sanctuary to visit a friend he'd met there—a brown eagle who was rescued after he lost a wing in a tragic accident. The relationship that Ken had with the eagle sprang from a spiritual connection. This connection gave Ken the Native American name KenBrownEagle, which he would carry proudly throughout the rest of his life, in this life.

*   *   *

It was very easy for Kenneth to fall in love with a face and a mind and personality. That's what happened with his feelings toward the director of *Scrooge*. He fell in love with everything about her. She was an excellent director, very professional and thorough.

Their relationship developed beyond that between a director and actor, at first with just a walk. Then New Year's was just around the corner, and they had a date and enjoyed the pleasure of each other's company on New Year's Eve, toasting to each other's well-being with a few glasses of champagne at Fifty-Ninth Street and Columbus Circle. They then saw the New Year come in together. It was a wonderful, enlightening experience.

Later, Roberta, who was a schoolteacher in addition to being a director, asked Ken if he would talk to her class about things they shouldn't do in life. He gladly said he would. Her students were inner-city children, and they were used to being around dealers and addicts and everything else that had to do with survival in the street world.

Ken walked through the school and into Roberta's classroom. He sat down and said good morning to the class. "My name is Ken," he told them, "and I'm here today as a friend of your teacher to talk to you about the negative effects of going in the fast lane in life. It's not going to work."

This one kid said, "I want to be like my uncle. He makes a lot of money."

"Yeah," Ken replied, "but if you follow the wrong path, there's no guarantee you'll live, and with cause and effect, your chances of success would be very slim. You wouldn't be free with your spirit and wouldn't be able to do what you want to do because you'd be in jail."

The child did understand what Ken said, and so did most of the rest of the class. For those who didn't understand, he explained again.

When it was all over, the students really seemed to appreciate him talking to them about why they shouldn't sell or take drugs or fall into the traps of a criminal lifestyle. He told them to continue in school and learn as much as they possibly could and to work toward positive results and achievements in life. It was yet another enlightening experience for Ken.

*   *   *

Ken liked to sit outside on the front stoop of the theater and talk to all the other members of the repertory company who were coming and going. He always made a kind gesture and acknowledged people passing by.

Ken was also involved with another project with the theater. A Japanese restaurant next door wanted to buy the building the theater was in in order to expand. The theatre, the oldest off-off-Broadway company in Manhattan, had been at that location for years, but the company didn't own the building but rented it. So everyone in the repertory company pledged to raise funds so the company could buy the building for good and stay there for many years to come. Being able to help was wonderful.

First, Ken dressed up in mime and went through the city wearing a sign on that said, "Please help save the 13th Street theatre." He didn't talk at all the whole day; it was a lot of fun! He mimicked people's walk or the style of their actions. He went to Central Park and sat with people, listening and learning without saying a word, and collected money for the theater.

In addition, Ken went back to his former contacts at the old sales accounts he'd had when he had sold mailing equipment and photo copiers. He asked the presidents, vice presidents, treasurers, or VPs of Operations to please donate to help save the 13th Street Repertory company and buy the building. Most of the companies did donate, giving him twenty-five, fifty, or a hundred dollars in cash or a check. It was really enlightening that he was able to go into the sales world with which he had been associated, mixing it with the theatre world, and accomplish something.

Ken very much enjoyed seeing all the shows at the theatre. His main goal was to learn as much as possible. He believed if he could put a little bit of different characters together all of in method acting, it was always an important study for Ken. That worked best for him. To get into character, he liked to be that character for awhile. Professor Fred was one of his most interesting and challenging roles.

One night on his way from the Mud Club, dancing all night, he saw one of the ladies of the evening out on the street walking on the same path he was on to get back home. He had seen this woman a few times before and had always greeted her with a hello. She asked him if he wanted a date. Ken replied, "Yeah I would love to go on a date, but I just want to make sure I have the right amount of cash on me."

"Okay, well, let me know," she said.

And he said he would.

That night came along. It had been a good day for sales. Ken was selling a lot of sweat suits and leg warmers at the time. A lot of his customers were dancers and streetwalkers, and they always bought from him also because they usually had cash. Finishing up his day, on his way home, he made a point to see the young lady walking again. This time as he approached her, he asked, "How about that date we spoke about before?"

"Sure I would like a date," she told him.

"Okay, let's go get a cab and I'll show you the theatre," he said, explaining where he lived and that he also performed in a lot of shows. "Come with me; let me show you the theatre and a favorite character I play."

So they got a cab and went to the theatre. Ken had a key, so he didn't have to wake anyone up. He showed her the lighting booth and the stage and the lobby with all the show posters and head shots of the actors. Then they went behind the stage, and Ken opened a trapdoor that had a ladder going downstairs, where costumes from some shows and props were stored.

"Have a seat," he told her. "I'll be right back."

When he came back, he was Professor Fred from *The Thing That Ate Syracuse* in complete costume and mask. He spoke very intelligently to the young lady with his deep professor's voice and mumbles. She looked in amazement at his transformation. They both enjoyed the evening together and had a fun, intimate time, even though Ken was the young lady's customer. He treated her like a lady, with the utmost respect. He didn't treat her like he was paying her for a date.

When it was time for her to go home, he called a cab for her. He paid her and paid the cabdriver for the fare. "I hope you enjoyed the evening with me," he said.

"Oh! I really had a great time," she told him. "Maybe we can do it again sometime."

"Maybe," Ken replied. "If it's supposed to be, it will be."

They said good-bye.

What a pleasant adventure, Ken thought to himself.

It had been a wonderful date—one that he would never forget. What was interesting as he thought about it was that he had never been shy before. And even though the woman had been a stranger he hadn't been shy with her. When he did a show, he was usually able to communicate his character and do his show properly in front of the audience, despite the butterflies in his stomach the first half a minute on stage. But after the show, when the cast went into the main lobby and met everybody from the audience, he would generally be very shy. He would frequently slip out another exit and be free, walking down the street. Even though he also found freedom acting on stage, he just had to break that barrier.

Something very important to Ken—something that would make him feel complete in the arts was to have a professional head shot. All of the actors and actresses had professional head shots. These shots showed the versatility in the faces and characters that he or she was portraying. Under the headlining for each show,was displayed in the lobby. the cast was listed, along with their pictures. He was going to get his first professional photo thanks to one of his actor friends who had played Murph opposite him in *The Indian Wants the Bronx*. This friend's mother was and is a professional photographer who does many head shots for people.

Another thought that had been speeding through his mind lately was that he was happy now, and he wasn't doing anything to cause his balance to be off, resulting in him drifting to the negative side. Even though he was positive, he knew that negative darkness could overtake you if you let it. You learned to spiritually condition and control yourself and maintain your self-disciplined balance.

He believed that his spirit had been here more than once. He didn't know exactly how many times, but during each lifetime—in whatever form of life he was in—he had improved and would continue to improve his spiritual balance. In other words, he would do better during each lifetime, with the guidance of the spirit and a higher power.

Walking and thinking about the past, present, and future, Ken's thoughts turned to Halloween, which was coming up. A party came to mind; he thought of going to, mostly with people in the arts world, in the SoHo District, where people from all areas of art lived, usually in big lofts. He decided that, for his costume, he would wear a black velvet blazer, a white shirt, black pants, and nice black dress shoes. Then he would put black makeup on one side of his face and white clown makeup on the other—half black and half white, like good and bad and yin and yang. That was unique to Ken, and it was also going to be fun and interesting at the party.

*   *   *

In the Shadow of Jorge Luis Borges was one of the most interesting and well-paying show-related jobs Ken had. However, he was a stage manager. The director from the 13th Street Repertory had recommended Ken for the job.

Being part of that production was an honor for Ken. It was at the University of the Streets Theatre in the lower east side of Manhattan. He had to give the actors their cues at precise moments throughout the show. That was an enlightening experience for Ken, and the theatre group gave Ken a nice little bio on the show program:

> Ken Thompson (Stage Manager) was born in Brooklyn in 1952. He first learned lighting at the Laurels Country Club as a teenager. He was Assistant Director and Lighting Technician at the Baders Residence for Adults in Spring Valley, N.Y. Currently, Ken is Stage Manager and Lighting Technician for the 13th Street Revue at the 13th Street Theatre. He studies acting with Ann Saxman and Gloria Kinter. He played Larry in "Our Dear Wife" at Studio R (Children's TV Experimental Workshop), the *cab driver* in "The Seekers" and *Peachy* in "The Emperor Laughs Back." He is currently appearing as *Professor Fred* in "The Thing That Ate Syracuse," a *Hindu-speaking Indian* in the world famous Israel Horovitz play "The Indian Wants the Bronx," and five different characters in "Snow White Show."

THE UNIVERSITY OF THE STREETS

Presents

IN THE SHADOW OF JORGE LUIS BORGES

A New Play Written and Directed by
S. Terry Gregory

NOV. 4-21

THURSDAY – SATURDAY 8:00 PM
SUNDAY 3:00 PM   RES: 254-9300

An Equity Approved Showcase

IN THE SHADOW OF JORGE LUIS BORGES

A New Play Written and Directed by
S. Terry Gregory

with

Kathleen Beck	Merriman Gatch *
Steve Lincoln *	Nina Howes
Greg Ragle	William J. Rosin
Susan A. San Pedro	Irma St. Paul
Nancy Santiago	Bruce H. Schultz
Barbara Weiss *	Panda Weiss
Ann Saxman *	Irene Shea

Paul Theobald

TED MORNEL	Production Manager
CRAIG HAFT	
PHIL ZACHS	Lighting
KEN THOMPSON	Stage Manager
SAADIA SALAHUDDEEN	
DONALD KVARES	Public Relations
ELSIE DRIGGS	Art
GEORGE JACOBS	Sound
LISA J. STEIN	Photography

The producers wish to express
special thanks to:

MAXIMO PRINTING and

GODDARD RIVERSIDE SENIOR CENTER

* appearing through the courtesy of
Actor's Equity Association

Ken Thompson

P.O. BOX 731
Quogue, Long Island
NY., NY. 11959
(516) 653-8754
(212) 724-2800

Height: 5'9"
Weight: 160 lbs.
D.O.B.: December 2, 1952
Baritone

Off-Off Broadway

Scrooge, Jacob Marley	13th Street Theatre, 1982-3
The Indian Wants the Bronx, Gupta	13th Street Theatre, 1982-3
The Thing that Ate Syracuse, Professor Fred	13th Street Theatre, 1982-3
Snow White, Woodsman,Prince	13th Street Theatre, 1982-3
The Empire Laughs Back, Peachy	13th Street Theatre, 1982
Our Dear Wife, Larry	Studio 2, Experimental
	T.V. Workshop 1979
The Seekers, Cab Driver	13th Street Theatre 1979

Film

The Warriors, gang member	1980
Captain Avenger, extra	1980

Staff/Tech

Assistant Director and Lighting Design, Hello Dolly, Baders Residence for Adults.	1982
Assistant Director, Snow White, 13th Street Theatre	1982
Stage Manager, In the Shadow of Luis Jorge Bourges, The University of the Streets Theatre	1982
Stage Manager and Lighting Design, The 13th Street Revue	1982
Lighting and Sound Technician, The Seekers, Line, Brother Theodore	1979
Lighting Technician, The Indian Wants the Bronx, 13th Street Theatre	1979
Lighting Technician, The Laurels Country Club and Resort	1968

Special Skills:Swimming, football, wrestling, track (running broad jump, 50 yard dash and 100 yard dash), archery, gymnastics (rings,rope and longhorse).

Other Career Experience

I've had extensive experience (since '975) in marketing and sales for the following companies: Ziff Davis Publishing Co., Dialogue Systems, Minolta Business Systems, Atlantic Photocopy, Friden Mailing Equipment

Ken wished that people in the arts had more and easier opportunities to be cast in film, TV, or commercial roles; they faced so many difficult obstacles when it came to getting into the unions, like SAG or Equity. Ken went through the steps in acting, even going so far as to live at the theater where he was performing. He didn't want to join the union just for the money. But for many, the choice to join or not to join eventually comes down to a matter of money. Ken didn't get paid for being in any of the off-off-Broadway productions in money, but he got paid with the reward of learning and increased knowledge of theatre and acting, among other things in theater.

While Ken stayed at the theatre, he became acquainted with the theater's piano player and composer, Ken Laufer, who also played piano for most of the shows Ken was in. Ken Laufer was a genius, and he always talked about making it further than just playing for almost every show at the theatre, including the 13th Street Revue. Ken always tried to motivate his friend and decided to try to be his artist representative. Ken believed in the piano player, and he had experience in corporate sales and marketing. For one of his attempts to get his friend booked, Ken wrote the following letter to the director of marketing at the Sheraton Mt. Royal Hotel in Montreal, Canada:

Dear Sir

I spoke with you recently by phone, and I am enclosing some material about a unique one-person "act." Something quite out of the ordinary: A *Mad Musical Evening with Ken Laufer*. Ken Laufer is a New York pianist and composer (masters from the Julliard School, 1966). His ragtime music is published and performed around the United States by Gunther Schuller and the New England Ragtime Ensemble. He has developed a humorous show involving virtuoso piano playing. It seems to get very enthusiastic response from every audience. He has been booked at Grossinqer's Country Club in Catskills, NY, ten times. Enclosed is a yellow sheet listing some of the bits in the show, but it is hard to really describe the effect of this very energetic, musical, and humorous piano playing, and the clever arrangements (for example, the "Flight of the Bumble Bee" played simultaneously with the "Sting"). Audiences at the improvisation (NYC) and NY Playboy Clubs (in 1980) went wild over the opening number, billed as the most amazing feat ever attempted at the piano: the entire musical output of the human race played in only five minutes. Another popular item is the Cockroach Marching Song, sung by zillions of cockroaches as they take over the world.

I hope this show (or a part of it) can be of service to you. Any additional information will gladly be sent.

Thank you for your kind attention.

Sincerely yours,
Ken Thompson
Artist representative

Ken mainly wrote the letter to boost his friend's morale, and he hoped a booking might result. He and the piano player were spiritual friends. They had known each other for a few years. Ken Laufer was an important part of the theater. He played for every show that had music in it. He always hung out with the cast members of different shows at the end of any given day, and everyone liked him. He was like a theater angel who was always there for the actors.

*   *   *

Ken's father's health started to decline, and handling all the responsibilities both in and out of the home became difficult for his stepmother. So Ken decided to move to Quogue and live with his parents and be there for them.

Before Ken left the 13th Street Repertory, the artistic director wrote a nice letter:

> To Whom It May Concern:
>
> Ken Thompson has been a member in good standing with our repertory company for the past three years. He has availed himself of all the learning possibilities here through classes, workshops and performances. He is serious and dedicated toward perfecting his craft and pursuing a career in theatre.
>
> Ken is also caring and helpful in whatever circumstances he is in.
>
> I recommend him highly to any group.
>
> Yours truly,
> Edith O'Hara
> Artistic Director

*   *   *

This is today, and hopefully there will be another tomorrow, to learn and follow the guidance life offers. Everyone has a higher power if he or she believes in one. That's why we were all given choices. Most people's higher power is God, called by many different names.

I'll tell you one thing—I'd rather be going up than down. I experienced the darkness, and now I just want to see the light. Because I changed, anyone can do it. Believe in your higher power to help and guide you. Trust me, spirituality and balance are the key essences in life.

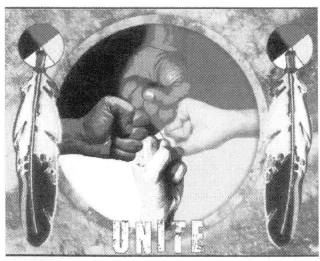

✹ Smithsonian

National Museum of the American Indian
Certifies the Registration of

HAROLD B. THOMPSON

on the HONOR WALL *of the*
NATIONAL MUSEUM OF THE AMERICAN INDIAN
The National Mall   Washington, D.C.

Lawrence M. Small
Secretary
SMITHSONIAN INSTITUTION

W. Richard West, Jr. (Southern Cheyenne)
Founding Director
NATIONAL MUSEUM OF THE AMERICAN INDIAN

May 19, 2006

Date Issued

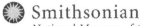

✺ Smithsonian

National Museum of the American Indian

Certifies the Registration of

KEN BROWN EAGLE

on the HONOR WALL *of the*

NATIONAL MUSEUM OF THE AMERICAN INDIAN

The National Mall   Washington, D.C.

Lawrence M. Small
Secretary
SMITHSONIAN INSTITUTION

W. Richard West, Jr. (Southern Cheyenne)
Founding Director
NATIONAL MUSEUM OF THE AMERICAN INDIAN

May 19, 2006

Date Issued